EDITH
WHARTON

AMERICAN WOMEN of ACHIEVEMENT

EDITH WHARTON

WILLIAM LEACH

CHELSEA HOUSE PUBLISHERS

NEW YORK • PHILADELPHIA

EDITOR-IN-CHIEF: Nancy Toff
EXECUTIVE EDITOR: Remmel T. Nunn
MANAGING EDITOR: Karyn Gullen Browne
COPY CHIEF: Perry Scott King
ART DIRECTOR: Giannella Garrett
PICTURE EDITOR: Elizabeth Terhune

Staff for EDITH WHARTON:

TEXT EDITOR: Marian W. Taylor
ASSISTANT EDITOR: Maria Behan
COPYEDITORS: Gillian Bucky, Sean Dolan
DESIGN: Design Oasis
PICTURE RESEARCH: Diane Wallis
PRODUCTION COORDINATOR: Alma Rodriguez
COVER ILLUSTRATION: Donna Day

CREATIVE DIRECTOR: Harold Steinberg

Printed and bound in the United States of America

3 5 7 9 8 6 4

Library of Congress Cataloging in Publication Data

Leach, William. EDITH WHARTON

(American women of achievement)
Bibliography: p.
Includes index.
1. Wharton, Edith, 1862–1937—Biography—Juvenile literature.
2. Authors, American—20th century—Biography—Juvenile
literature. [1. Wharton, Edith, 1862–1937. 2. Authors, American]
I. Title. II. Series.
PS3545.H16Z694   1987   813'.52 [B] [92]   87-5203

ISBN 1-55546-682-6
    0-7910-0425-2 (pbk.)

C O N T E N T S

AMERICAN WOMEN of ACHIEVEMENT

Abigail Adams
women's rights advocate

Jane Addams
social worker

Louisa May Alcott
author

Marian Anderson
singer

Susan B. Anthony
woman suffragist

Ethel Barrymore
actress

Clara Barton
*founder of the American
Red Cross*

Elizabeth Blackwell
physician

Nellie Bly
journalist

Margaret Bourke-White
photographer

Pearl Buck
author

Rachel Carson
biologist and author

Mary Cassatt
artist

Agnes De Mille
choreographer

Emily Dickinson
poet

Isadora Duncan
dancer

Amelia Earhart
aviator

Mary Baker Eddy
*founder of the Christian
Science church*

Betty Friedan
feminist

Althea Gibson
tennis champion

Emma Goldman
political activist

Helen Hayes
actress

Lillian Hellman
playwright

Katharine Hepburn
actress

Karen Horney
psychoanalyst

Anne Hutchinson
religious leader

Mahalia Jackson
gospel singer

Helen Keller
humanitarian

Jeane Kirkpatrick
diplomat

Emma Lazarus
poet

Clare Boothe Luce
author and diplomat

Barbara McClintock
biologist

Margaret Mead
anthropologist

Edna St. Vincent Millay
poet

Julia Morgan
architect

Grandma Moses
painter

Louise Nevelson
sculptor

Sandra Day O'Connor
Supreme Court justice

Georgia O'Keeffe
painter

Eleanor Roosevelt
diplomat and humanitarian

Wilma Rudolph
champion athlete

Florence Sabin
medical researcher

Beverly Sills
opera singer

Gertrude Stein
author

Gloria Steinem
feminist

Harriet Beecher Stowe
author and abolitionist

Mae West
entertainer

Edith Wharton
author

Phillis Wheatley
poet

Babe Didrikson Zaharias
champion athlete

CHELSEA HOUSE PUBLISHERS

"Remember the Ladies"

MATINA S. HORNER

Remember the Ladies." That is what Abigail Adams wrote to her husband John, then a delegate to the Continental Congress, as the Founding Fathers met in Philadelphia to form a new nation in March of 1776. "Be more generous and favorable to them than your ancestors. Do not put such unlimited power in the hands of the Husbands. If particular care and attention is not paid to the Ladies," Abigail Adams warned, "we are determined to foment a Rebellion, and will not hold ourselves bound by any Laws in which we have no voice, or Representation."

The words of Abigail Adams, one of the earliest American advocates of women's rights, were prophetic. Because when we have not "remembered the ladies," they have, by their words and deeds, reminded us so forcefully of the omission that we cannot fail to remember them. For the history of American women is as interesting and varied as the history of our nation as a whole. American women have played an integral part in founding, settling, and building our country. Some we remember as remarkable women who—against great odds—achieved distinction in the public arena: Anne Hutchinson, who in the 17th century became a charismatic religious leader; Phillis Wheatley, an 18th-century black slave who became a poet; Susan B. Anthony, whose name is synonymous with the 19th-century women's rights movement, and who led the struggle to enfranchise women; and, in our own century, Amelia Earhart, the first woman to cross the Atlantic Ocean by air.

These extraordinary women certainly merit our admiration, but other women, "common women," many of them all but forgotten, should also be recognized for their contributions to American thought and culture. Women have been community builders; they have founded schools and formed voluntary associations to help those in need; they have assumed the major responsibility for rearing children, passing on from one generation to the next the values that keep a culture alive. These and innumerable other contributions, once ignored, are now being recognized by scholars, students, and the public. It is exciting and gratifying to realize that a part of our history that was hardly acknowledged a few generations ago is now being studied and brought to light.

In recent decades, the field of women's history has grown from obscurity to a politically controversial splinter movement to academic respectability, in many cases mainstreamed into such traditional disciplines as history, economics, and psychology. Scholars of women, both female and male, have organized research centers at such prestigious institutions as Wellesley College, Stanford University, and the University of California. Other notable centers for women's studies are the Center for the American Woman and Politics at the Eagleton Institute of Politics at Rutgers University, the Henry A. Murray Research Center for the Study of Lives, at Radcliffe College, and the Women's Research and Education Institute, the research arm of the Congressional Caucus on Women's Issues. Other scholars and public figures have established archives and libraries, such as the Schlesinger Library on the History of Women in America, at Radcliffe College, and the Sophia Smith Collection, at Smith College, to collect and preserve the written and tangible legacies of women.

From the initial donation of the Women's Rights Collection in 1943, the Schlesinger Library grew to encompass vast collections documenting the manifold accomplishments of American women. Simultaneously, the women's movement in general and the academic discipline of women's studies in particular also began with a narrow definition and gradually expanded their mandate. Early causes such as woman suffrage and social reform, abolition and organized labor were joined by newer concerns such as the history of women in business and the professions and in politics and government; the study of the family; and social issues such as health policy and education.

Women, as historian Arthur M. Schlesinger, jr., once pointed out, "have constituted the most spectacular casualty of traditional history. They have made up at least half the human race, but you could never tell that by looking at the books historians write." The new breed of historians is remedying that omission. They have written books about immigrant women and about working-class women who struggled for survival in cities and about black women who met the challenges of life in rural areas. They are telling the stories of women who, despite the barriers of tradition and economics, became lawyers and doctors and public figures.

The women's studies movement has also led scholars to question traditional interpretations of their respective disciplines. For example, the study of war has traditionally been an exercise in military and political analysis, an examination of strategies planned and executed by men. But scholars of women's history have pointed out that wars have also been periods of tremendous change and even opportunity for women, because the very absence of men on the home front enabled them to expand their educational, economic, and professional activities and to assume leadership in their homes.

The early scholars of women's history showed a unique brand of courage in choosing to investigate new subjects and take new approaches to old ones. Often, like their subjects, they endured criticism and even ostracism by their academic colleagues. But their efforts have unquestionably been worthwhile, because with the publication of each new study and book another piece of the historical patchwork is sewn into place, revealing an increasingly comprehensive picture of the role of women in our rich and varied history.

Such books on groups of women are essential, but books that focus on the lives of individuals are equally indispensable. Biographies can be inspirational, offering their readers the example of people with vision who have looked outside themselves for their goals and have often struggled against great obstacles to achieve them. Marian Anderson, for instance, had to overcome racial bigotry in order to perfect her art and perform as a concert singer. Isadora Duncan defied the rules of classical dance to find true artistic freedom. Jane Addams had to break down society's notions of the proper role for women in order to create new social institutions, notably the settlement house. All of these women had to come to terms both with themselves and with the world in which they lived. Only then could they move ahead as pioneers in their chosen callings.

Biography can inspire not only by adulation but also by realism. It helps us to see not only the qualities in others that we hope to emulate, but also, perhaps, the weaknesses that made them "human." By helping us identify with the subject on a more personal level they help us to feel that we, too, can achieve such goals. We read about Eleanor Roosevelt, for instance, who occupied a unique and seemingly enviable position as the wife of the president. Yet we can sympathize with her inner dilemma: an inherently shy woman, she had to force herself to live a most public life in order to use her position to benefit others. We may not be able to imagine ourselves having the immense poetic talent of Emily Dickinson, but from her story we can understand the challenges faced by a creative woman who was expected to fulfill many family responsibilities. And though few of us will ever reach the level of athletic accomplishment displayed by Wilma Rudolph or Babe Zaharias, we can still appreciate their spirit, their overwhelming will to excel.

A biography is a multifaceted lens. It is first of all a magnification, the intimate examination of one particular life. But at the same time, it is a wide-angle lens, informing us about the world in which the subject lived. We come away from reading about one life knowing more about the social, political, and economic fabric of the time. It is for this reason, perhaps, that the great New England essayist Ralph Waldo Emerson wrote, in 1841, "There is properly no history: only biography." And it is also why biography, and particularly women's biography, will continue to fascinate writers and readers alike.

EDITH WHARTON

Born into a wealthy New York City family in 1862, Edith Jones (shown here in 1870) loved books, but she grew up in a society that considered education for young women unnecessary.

ONE

A Sea of Wonders

On a bright winter day in 1872, 10-year-old Edith Jones prepared to enter a room that had long been forbidden to her. The prospect filled her with more excitement than she had ever known; her large brown eyes gleamed with anticipation.

The room was a small one on the ground floor of Edith's home in New York City. Heavy green curtains framed the windows. Sunlight streamed over the thick Oriental carpet that covered the floor. Dominating the room was a huge fireplace whose oak-wood mantelpiece rested on the heads of carved wooden knights. Along the walls were oak shelves protected by glass doors and filled with hundreds of beautifully bound books that Edith had never seen before.

Edith's parents had just given her permission to enter a new world: her father's library. Once she stepped over the threshold and experienced the treasures within, her life would be changed forever.

For some children, longing for spectacular adventures, such an event would have meant very little. For Edith, however, entering this room was like discovering a magical place—a "sea of wonders," as she later described it. "I was enthralled with words," she said. "Wherever I went, they sang to me like birds in an enchanted forest."

Edith had been inventing her own stories since she was six years old; now, in her father's library, she was surrounded by grown-up storytellers, hundreds of them! Day after day, she disappeared into the once-forbidden room; there, kneeling on the richly patterned carpet, she would slide open the glass doors and pull out one vol-

The consuming passion of Lucretia Rhinelander Jones's life was beautiful clothes. Thirty-seven years old when her daughter Edith was born, Jones proved to be a cold and distant mother.

ume after another. And what magnificent stories they held!

Edith plunged happily into the work of such great poets as Milton, Coleridge, Shelley, Dante, and Keats. By the time she was 15, she had read every word of the poems and plays of the famous German writer Goethe, all of Shakespeare's plays, and much of the Bible. She read books and essays on architecture and art, on philosophy and history. Bizarre people and exotic animals marched across the pages, filling her head with visions. She fantasized about becoming a writer herself.

Edith grew to love the room that contained these books. It was her own secret retreat, a place apart from everything else she knew. Here she could think and act like an adult (not, as she said later, like a "mere little girl"). Here no one, not even her parents, intruded. Not until years later did Edith speak about the wonders she discovered in the library.

Far from being pleased to find that Edith had developed into a passionate reader, her parents were worried about her. They thought she was spending too much time with books. Indeed, apart from letting their daughter into the library, Edith's mother and father, who were very wealthy, did almost nothing to educate her.

Although Edith had a governess (a woman who took care of her), she had no tutors; nor did she have any books

George Frederic Jones was 22 when he married 19-year-old Lucretia Rhinelander in 1844. Edith, the couple's third and last child, was born 18 years later.

of her own. Her two older brothers studied at Cambridge University in England, but Edith never attended school or college.

She had been born into a time when girls of her class were not expected to be educated, to work, or to think very deeply about anything. Girls were expected to be "nice"—polite, fashionable, and pretty. Well-to-do women of Edith's generation were urged only to marry, to have babies, and to entertain elegantly.

Like most of the era's fashionable homes, Lucretia Jones's Manhattan town house was swathed in heavy draperies and crammed with ornate furniture, chandeliers, and decorative objects.

Lucretia Jones, Edith's mother, was famous for her beautiful clothes and stylish parties. She became particularly distressed by the direction her daughter's intellectual life was taking. She came to view the library as a threat to Edith's proper development. Both subtly and openly, she ridiculed Edith's "affectations," her use of "big words," her passion for "making up" stories (nice women did not write books), and her reading habits.

Finally, Edith's mother decreed that her daughter could not read any novel in the library without asking for permission. Dutifully (and until she was 23 years old) Edith brought every novel she wanted to read to her mother's attention; Lucretia Jones frequently ruled the books "unsuitable" and ordered them returned to the shelves.

In the 1870s young women from wealthy New York families were just starting to have "coming-out" parties

Coachmen drive their carriages along New York's Fifth Avenue in 1875. Edith Jones and her family lived in a three-story house at Fifth and 23rd Street, a mile south of this scene.

in glittering ballrooms. At these events, relatives and friends would gather to dance, dine, and "introduce" the girls to society. Edith's parents tried to slow the growth of her literary interests by speeding up her social debut. This meant that Edith, at the age of 17, was to become a debutante.

She arrived at her party in 1879 wearing a low-necked blouse of pale green brocade and a white muslin skirt. She carried a bouquet of lilies of the valley.

Shy and nervous, she huddled close to her mother, declining invitations to dance, speaking to no one.

Edith's pained reaction to her debut is easy to understand. By becoming a debutante, she was symbolically announcing to the world that she was ready to give up her independence and her "sea of wonders." She was exchanging her hopes of becoming a writer for the role of a secure and traditional wife.

Tensely clutching her long white gloves, 14-year-old Edith Jones prepares to receive family guests. Although she preferred reading books to attending parties, Edith tried to do what was expected of her.

Although Edith would marry one day, she resented being forced to undergo this "coming-out" experience. Even more deeply, she resented her lack of childhood education and the fact that no one acknowledged her for what she was—a creative person who loved words and books and yearned for knowledge.

Edith would always remember that sun-filled day when she was given the freedom of her father's library. Her mind, she later said, "would have starved" without it. The library ignited her imagination. She dreamed of writing novels like those her mother forbade her to read, and in spite of her family's opposition, she never lost touch with that dream. Years later, in fact, Edith would become one of the greatest novelists America has ever produced.

Edith Wharton, always fond of dogs, cuddles one of her favorites in the early 1880s. A shy and lonely child, she felt closer to her pets than to most of the people she knew.

TWO

A Lonely Childhood

Edith Newbold Jones was born in her parents' Manhattan house on January 24, 1862. Her mother, Lucretia Rhinelander Jones, and her father, George Jones, belonged to wealthy and aristocratic New York families whose ancestries dated back to the American Revolution.

Lucretia Jones's family background was especially well stocked with ambitious and successful men. They had made fortunes in shipbuilding and foreign trade and had gotten even richer by investing in New York City real estate.

By 1900 Edith's grandfather, William Rhinelander, had amassed an estate valued at $50 million—an amount worth even more then than it would be today. The Jones family lived in luxury on the income from this inheritance. Servants were plentiful; no

family members—including George Jones—did any work.

Edith's parents were among the "best" New York families—people who mingled only with one another and who shared the same strict standards of social conduct. On the whole, they were honest and decent individuals, notable for their good manners and good taste.

They tended, however, to be stuffy and narrow-minded, hostile to intellectual life, to art and literature, to innovation of any kind. If a member of their group—particularly a young woman—did anything extraordinary, cared for the "wrong" people, or expressed herself passionately about anything, she was laughed at, scorned, or avoided.

George and Lucretia Jones spent most of their evenings entertaining, or

Vacationers enjoy Newport's beach in the 1870s. A relaxed summer colony during Edith Wharton's childhood, the Rhode Island town was later the site of elaborate mansions and social activities.

being entertained by, their friends. Sometimes they went to the opera, not because they loved music but because it was a fashionable pastime. In the summers the family vacationed at their home in Newport, an expensive Rhode Island resort town that attracted the rich and wellborn.

In Newport Edith and her brothers went boating, played tennis and croquet, and flirted with other young people of their own class. Lucretia Jones received visitors and paid calls in her elegant and expensive gowns.

When Edith was four years old, her parents took her and her brothers on a European "grand tour," a common practice of wealthy American families of the time. On the tour—which lasted for six years—Edith learned Italian, German, and French.

Edith loved Rome. She was delighted by the abundance of violets, daffodils, and tulips on the hills outside the city and dazzled by the sight of Roman Catholic cardinals passing by in gilded

Horse-drawn traffic makes its leisurely way through late 19th-century Manhattan. Edith Wharton would set several novels in "Old New York," as she called the city of her childhood.

Punctuated by the Seine River and its many ornate bridges, Paris today looks much as it did when Edith Wharton first visited — and fell in love with — the French capital in the 1860s.

coaches, their scarlet and gold robes flashing in the sun. She began to develop a deep love of beauty, but she kept such feelings strictly to herself.

Paris provided Edith with her greatest pleasures. Here she learned to dance, and here her father taught her the alphabet. It was in Paris that she "made up" her first stories about "real people." She was not yet able to read, but she invented a wonderful game.

Pacing through her parents' parlor,

she would hold a book, turning its pages while she recited tales from her own imagination. She later recalled being "swept off on a sea of dreams" as she told her stories. It is not surprising that, as an adult, she decided to live in Paris, the city where she began to think as a writer.

On the surface, Edith Jones was a lucky little girl. She had a luxurious home, the chance to travel, and no responsibilities. But Edith was not happy. She was sure her mother did not love her—and Edith had good reasons.

After the birth of her sons, Lucretia Jones had planned to have no more children. By the time Edith was born, the boys were teenagers, and Lucretia was 37. Edith's entry into the world was a decidedly unwelcome event; as the child grew up, her mother treated her more and more coldly. Lucretia Jones was unpredictable, but she could be counted on to sneer at anything Edith treasured. She made fun of her daughter's large hands and feet; Edith was painfully self-conscious about these "defects" for the rest of her life.

When Edith was 12, she wrote her first story. "'Oh, how do you do, Mrs. Brown?' said Mrs. Temples," the story began. "'If only I had known you were going to call, I should have tidied up the drawing room.'" Shyly, Edith showed the story to her mother. Lucretia Jones dismissed it with a sniff. "Drawing rooms are *always* tidy," she said.

Edith's mother went even further to show her disapproval of such activity: she refused to let her daughter have any paper to write on. "For lack of paper," Edith recalled later, "I was driven to begging for the wrappings of parcels delivered at the house." She always kept a stack in her room.

Edith tried to find comfort in her fa-

Doyley (Hannah Doyle), the nurse who took care of Edith Jones, was utterly devoted to her young charge. Edith returned her affection, regarding the kindly Irishwoman as her best friend.

ther. He was a gentle man, but he was busy with his social life and had little time to listen to a little girl. Edith's Irish nurse, Doyley, was genuinely fond of her, but her affection could not compensate for Lucretia Jones's rejection. Relatives and family friends were no help, either; they prized conformity above all things and detested the expression of strong feelings.

Edith grew up expecting pain and disappointment. She thought of herself as a small, helpless creature. Why, she wondered, did her mother dislike her? What had she done to deserve such coldness? Perhaps as a result of her lonely childhood, she had a lifelong compassion for all defenseless beings. Any creature—human or animal—treated with neglect or cruelty would always stir deep wells of sympathy in her.

Edith often dreamed of ghosts and wolves. When she was nine, she almost died of typhoid fever. During her convalescence, her nightmares intensified, and her fear of the "formless horrors" that had peopled her dreams remained long after she was fully recovered. She was sure something was threatening her, that something awful lurked in every shadow.

Her worst hours came when she returned home after her daily walks. Always, at the door of her house, she sensed a dreadful, icy presence, ready to fall upon her and crush her. When she was middle-aged, Edith would write bloodcurdling tales of the supernatural, but not until she was 28 years old would she sleep in the same room with a book of ghost stories. And not until then could she shake the fear that always overcame her at the door of her mother's house.

As Edith grew up, she concealed her true feelings about most things, trying hard to meet her mother's expectations and to conform to the standards of her class. She imitated the fashionable girls she met. She went to parties

TALES OF MEN AND GHOSTS

BY

EDITH WHARTON

Published in 1910, this collection of stories sprang from Wharton's own childhood fears. The "teller" of such tales, she said in the book's preface, "should be well frightened in the telling."

and to great balls, often waltzing until 3 o'clock in the morning. Determined to do the "right thing," she began to think about marriage.

By the time she was 21, she had met three potential husbands. The first was Harry Stevens, a rich young man whose life was firmly controlled by his mother. He asked Edith Jones to marry him, and she accepted. His mother, however, made it clear that she disapproved of the match, and so the wedding was, as the newspaper society pages reported, "postponed indefinitely"—a polite way of saying it would never take place.

The second possibility was Walter Berry, a tall, lanky Harvard graduate. Cultivated and intelligent, he was unlike most of the men Edith Jones had known. The two liked each other as soon as they met; they talked vaguely of marriage but never made any definite commitment. Many years later, Berry would become one of Edith's closest friends.

She met the third candidate at Newport in the summer of 1883. Another Harvard man, 33-year-old Edward Robbins Wharton had much to recommend him. Like Edith Jones, he loved to travel. He was good-looking, boyishly charming, fond of nature and animals.

He was, on the other hand, rather unimaginative. Bored by art and literature, he preferred good wines to good

Embarrassed by her "large" hands, 18-year-old Edith Wharton hides them in this 1880 portrait. Edith's self-consciousness about her hands and feet was the result of her mother's frequent ridicule.

27

conversation. He was rich and well bred, the product of upper-class families from Virginia and Massachusetts. Like George Jones, he did not work, and he had no desire to find a vocation. Lucretia Jones decided he was the perfect man for her daughter. Soon after he had arrived in Newport, she gave an elaborate dinner party in his honor.

"Teddy" Wharton was in no hurry to give up his carefree bachelor life, but Lucretia Jones was a determined woman. In the spring of 1885—twenty months and many dinner parties later—Wharton asked Edith Jones to marry him. She still longed for a life in which intellectual and artistic matters played a large role, but she had come to believe such a goal was impossible. She accepted Wharton's proposal.

Three years earlier, George Jones, Edith's father, had died after a long illness. Invitations to the Wharton-Jones wedding were sent out by the mother of the bride-to-be. They read, "Mrs. George Frederic Jones requests the honour of your presence at the marriage of her daughter to Mr. Edward R. Wharton, at Trinity Chapel, on Wednesday April Twenty-ninth at twelve o'clock." Interestingly, the invitations mentioned the mother's name but not the bride's.

The minister who performed the ceremony was a widely known opponent of "intellectual emancipation" for women. In his wedding sermon, he said that the only purpose of educating a woman was to prepare her for marriage. All wives, he said solemnly, should expect to sacrifice their own needs and interests to the comfort and well-being of their husbands. It was, in all respects, a completely traditional wedding for 1885.

Edith Wharton's marriage was a disaster from the beginning. At 23 she knew nothing about sexual relationships. She had no idea what to expect from marriage, a common dilemma for "proper" young women in the 19th century. She recalled later that, two days before the wedding, she had finally gotten the courage to ask her mother "what marriage was really like."

Lucretia Jones was horrified. "I never heard such a ridiculous question!" she snapped. The anxious daughter persisted. "I'm afraid, Mamma—I want to know what will happen to me." This time her mother responded with open contempt: "You've seen enough pictures and statues in your life," she said. "Haven't you noticed that men are . . . made differently from women?"

When her daughter nodded shyly, Lucretia Jones apparently decided she had done her duty as a mother. "Then for heaven's sake," she said, "don't ask me any more silly questions. You can't be as stupid as you pretend."

Edith Jones had always had trouble in establishing intimate, trusting rela-

Among the relatives flanking Lucretia Jones (seated) at her Newport summer home in 1884 are her future son-in-law, "Teddy" Wharton (right), and her daughter, Edith (standing at right).

The new Mrs. Edward Wharton wears a bustle, the height of fashion in 1885. Although friends often admired her red-gold hair and expressive brown eyes, Wharton thought of herself as "plain."

tionships with others. That difficulty now combined with fear and ignorance to make a satisfactory sexual alliance with her husband impossible. Judging from hints in *A Backward Glance*, the autobiography Edith Wharton wrote in 1934, she and Teddy Wharton had an almost nonexistent sex life.

In her memoirs, Edith Wharton blamed her childlessness on her mother. Lucretia Jones's withholding of sexual information, said her daughter, "did more than anything else to falsify and misdirect my whole life." Wharton got over her sexual trauma eventually, but by then her marriage was in ruins.

Teddy Wharton was genuinely fond of his wife, and he tried to be companionable. He remained, however, completely uninterested in the things that mattered most to her. His persistent indifference to the arts left her feeling stifled, even though she had finally escaped her mother's house. Edith Wharton felt imprisoned by both her past and her present.

Wharton is joined by two of her adored dogs in this 1890 portrait. She once listed the "ruling passions" of her life; the first three were "justice and order," "dogs," and "books."

THREE

Mrs. Edward Wharton

Edith Newbold Jones Wharton was determined to become a writer, whether her husband and family disapproved or not. She had a deep-seated need to build a bridge to others through words, to reach out through the beauty of language. It was a need too strong to be conquered.

For the first few years of her marriage, she wrote very little. In 1889, however, she submitted a poem to *Scribner's* magazine. When she learned it had been accepted for publication in the magazine's October issue, she was thrilled. The $20 payment she received was not important to a wealthy woman like Wharton, but the recognition was. "As long as I live, I shall never forget my sensations," she wrote later. "I was to appear in print!"

Encouraged, she sent another offering to *Scribner's*. Entitled "Mrs. Man- stey's View," it was a short story about an aging woman whose only joy in life—the garden she can see from her New York boardinghouse window—is threatened by the construction of a new building next door. The editor of *Scribner's* liked this, too. He ran it in the magazine in the spring of 1890, becoming the first person to publish a work of fiction by Edith Wharton.

In 1888 Wharton learned that a distant relative had died, leaving her a substantial legacy. Now completely secure financially, she bought a small town house in Manhattan and a large home, complete with stables and extensive formal gardens, in Newport. She had become increasingly interested in architecture and interior design, and she turned her energies toward renovating and decorating both places.

Pencraig, the Jones's Newport house, was tiny in comparison to some of its gigantic neighbors. Early in their marriage, Edith and Teddy Wharton lived in a cottage on Pencraig's grounds.

Home design turned out to be an enthusiasm shared by both Whartons. Teddy Wharton had a good eye for structural detail and, his wife discovered, surprisingly good taste in decorating. The couple worked on the reshaping of their new houses with Ogden Codman, a gifted young Boston architect. The three enjoyed their collaboration, and Codman and Edith Wharton soon decided to write a book together about home design.

This was a subject with which she was completely comfortable; she had an almost mystical feeling about houses, and she knew a great deal about them. All through her life, she wrote later, they held a magical fascination for her. Some houses, especially those that were old and intricately constructed, affected her almost as if they were human. Depending on who had lived in them over the years, she thought of them as kind and warm or as stern and cruel.

Just as she compared houses with

people, Wharton drew parallels between people and houses. Some individuals, she thought, were like big, unlocked homes; they were open, friendly, easy to be with. She saw other people as complex, full of nooks and crannies, having many rooms that were hard to find. More women than men, according to Wharton's theories, had these hidden rooms.

Despite the appearance in print of her work, Wharton had only the most fragile confidence in herself as a writer. She was depressed by the lack of interest in her writing shown by those closest to her. She often suffered from headaches, intense fatigue, and nausea. Today, Wharton's ailments might be diagnosed as psychosomatic—arising from emotional rather than physical disorders. Whatever their cause, they made her miserable.

The turning point in her life came in 1897, when she sent the rough manuscript of the book she and Codman had written to her editor at *Scribner's* magazine. Impressed, he passed it along to Scribners's book division. Publisher Charles Scribner was not convinced that a book about houses would make much money, but after asking them for substantial revising and polishing, he agreed to print it.

Now that she had a book assignment, Wharton set to work. She soon discovered that organizing the material she and Codman had collected was a

Publisher Charles Scribner, who accepted Edith Wharton's first book — The Decoration of Houses — *in 1897, released 18 more Wharton titles over the next 25 years.*

more complicated task than she had expected. At this point, Walter Berry, the man Wharton had almost married 14 years earlier, arrived in Newport. The two quickly resumed their friendship. In the years to come, they would again be separated for long periods, but their close, affectionate relationship would last a lifetime.

Berry was a lawyer by profession but a scholar by inclination. His deepest interest was literature. He was the first person to take an interest in Wharton's writing. He analyzed, criticized, and praised her work. As good friends will,

A 1902 publicity photograph of America's newest best-selling author is captioned: "Mrs. Edith Wharton, author of The Valley of Decision, *one of the successes of the season."*

he gave her confidence and urged her to write as she felt, not as she thought others expected her to feel.

With Berry's guidance, Wharton finished her book in 1897. Entitled *The Decoration of Houses*, it was one of the first books about home design ever published in the United States. It offered detailed information and advice on everything from ceilings and walls to libraries and bathrooms. It was extremely critical of the overcrowded, stuffy rooms that were then much in favor. These were the kind of rooms in which Wharton had grown up, the kind her mother liked. Wharton, however, had always felt suffocated in such surroundings.

Scribners released 1,000 copies of *The Decoration of Houses*. To the surprise of both the publisher and the authors, every copy was quickly snapped up. The book went back to press and continued to sell steadily for years. Encouraged by its success, Wharton began to write feverishly. In the first few months of 1898 she produced seven short stories, including "Souls Belated," which many critics consider one of her best works of fiction.

By 1899 Wharton had completed several stories, which Scribners published under the title of *The Greater Inclination*. Offering the world a book of fiction was a giant step for the budding author. She was not at all sure about the quality of her stories. On pins and needles, she waited to see if anyone would praise it.

Then, as Wharton put it later, "the incredible happened." Readers and critics not only praised the book; they raved about it. Reviews brimmed with such phrases as "literary genius," "rare creative power," and "exquisite craftsmanship." From New York to London to Paris, thousands of readers bought and admired *The Greater Inclination*.

Marble House was one of the many fantastic "cottages" built by Newport millionaires in the 1890s. Edith Wharton had loved the "old" Newport, but she detested its new aura of showy wealth.

The Whartons selected Lenox, Massachusetts, for the site of their new home, The Mount. Earlier literary residents of Lenox had included Nathaniel Hawthorne and Herman Melville.

Wharton felt a sensation of power, something she had never experienced before.

She had suddenly stepped onto the public stage as an accomplished writer of fiction. She had found her vocation: she was—as she had always dreamed of being—a professional storyteller. At the age of 37, Wharton finally felt like an independent adult. The cloud of depression that had so often shadowed her life lifted.

Flushed with her success, Wharton began writing her first novel. She was now the same age her mother had been at the time of her daughter's birth. From this point on, Wharton would give birth herself, not to children but to books. She would write novels like those her mother had forbidden her to read so long ago.

Lucretia Jones had moved to Paris in 1893. Although she was to make a number of thinly disguised appearances in

The Mount's library, like all its other rooms, was designed by Edith Wharton. She also enjoyed managing the great house. "I am," she once told a friend, "rather a housekeeperish person."

Wharton's fiction, she played a very small part in her daughter's life after she left the United States. Wharton paid brief calls on her in Paris in 1899 and 1900, but she no longer kept up any pretense of daughterly affection. When Jones, then 76 years old, died in 1901, Wharton made a few references to "my poor mother," but it was clear she was not deeply grieved by the death of this distant, stern, and chilly matriarch.

For the first 15 years of their marriage, the Whartons divided their time between their home in Newport and trips to Europe. Newport had always attracted wealthy families, but during Wharton's childhood, these people had lived simply, in comfortable but unpretentious homes. By the 1890s more and more of the "new rich"—fabulously wealthy people whose tastes ran to palatial houses and extravagant entertainments—had settled

Walter Berry was one of the most important people in Edith Wharton's life. A lifelong bachelor, he served as her literary adviser, traveling companion, confidant, and cherished friend.

in the Rhode Island seaside town.

Teddy Wharton loved the glittering atmosphere of "modern" Newport, but his wife much preferred the quiet life Newport had offered in earlier times. She had also decided that Newport's damp seacoast air was unhealthy.

Teddy Wharton's mother and sister had a summer home in Lenox, a small resort town in the rolling Berkshire Hills of western Massachusetts. The younger Whartons had often visited the family there, and in 1901 Edith Wharton decided it was the perfect lo-

cation for a new house. She had long wanted a home of her own design, a place where she could write free of interruption and away from what she called "the inanities of Newport." She was sure the fresh mountain air would be good for her health, her writing career, and her husband.

Wharton may have wanted to escape the showy "cottages"—which were more like castles—of Newport, but the house she built in Lenox was hardly a model of simplicity. The Mount, as she called the new place, was modeled after an immense English manor house designed by the famous 17th-century English architect Christopher Wren.

Overlooking a wooded lake, The Mount had separate suites for its owners, a series of elegant guest rooms, and space for 12 live-in servants. The huge, high-ceilinged ground-floor rooms were surrounded by broad terraces leading to intricately laid out gardens, a stable, and a greenhouse. Both the Whartons were delighted with the house. Here they entertained friends, rode their horses, and relaxed. And here Edith Wharton completed her first novel.

The Valley of Decision, an 18th-century historical romance, is set in Italy, a country Wharton adored. The book's theme is one that always appealed to her: the struggle to hold onto the most valuable things of the past while em-

Edward (Teddy) Wharton displays an armful of dogs in 1886. Devoted to animals, he never allowed the chickens, sheep, or cows he raised at The Mount to be slaughtered for food.

Holding one of her ever-present dogs in her lap, Wharton scans a new novel in 1897. Although she loved most animals, there were some exceptions: she once defined a cat as "a snake in furs."

reviewer, "will undoubtedly become a classic." A Chicago critic called the novel "the most distinguished performance yet accomplished on this continent." From Louisville, Kentucky, came the opinion that *Valley* was "the most splendid achievement of an American man or woman in fiction."

Wharton's writing brought her more than fame. Just as she had always dreamed it would, it formed a bridge to other people. She began to make the kind of friends she had always wanted to have, people who, as she put it, "lived for the things I had always secretly longed for."

She dreamed of creating a small community of people who shared her deep love for literature and art. These "happy few" would, she believed, become a true "republic of the spirit." In her opinion, a truly admirable individual was open-minded and cosmopolitan, free from prejudice, and eager to embrace life's wonderful possibilities. For the rest of her life, Wharton would seek out such people, often traveling great distances to be with them.

Edith Wharton had an extraordinary capacity for friendship. One of her great friends was Walter Berry; another was Howard Sturgis, a wealthy American bachelor who lived in London and who hoped to become a successful writer. Tall, dark-eyed, and powerfully built, Sturgis spent most of his abundant spare time on an unusual hobby:

bracing the best of the present. It is not Wharton's best novel, but it was a huge success when it was published in 1902.

Readers everywhere heaped praise on *Valley*. The book, said a New York

Accompanied by a pair of Wharton pets, two of Wharton's good friends, eccentric wit Howard Sturgis (left) and French novelist Paul Bourget, share a quiet moment at The Mount.

needlework. He knitted, crocheted, and embroidered all day long. He delighted Wharton with his wit, high spirits, and wide-ranging conversation.

Wharton's most rewarding association may have been her friendship with Henry James, author of some of the finest novels in the English language. She particularly admired such James novels as *The American* and *The Portrait of a Lady*. The two novelists shared the same outlook on life, the same unyielding devotion to the craft of writing, the same love of language.

James and Wharton had crossed paths on several social occasions in the late 1880s, but she had made little impression on him. In 1902, however, he read *The Valley of Decision* and recognized an exceptional talent. He sent her a copy of his own latest novel, *The Wings of the Dove*, along with a letter.

The letter was full of praise for *The Valley of Decision*, which he called "brilliant." It was also full of advice. He urged her to write novels about her own country in her own time rather than about faraway places in the past. "Do New York!" he said. "The firsthand account is precious." James's letter concluded with an invitation to visit him.

In 1903, when the two writers met at James's home in England, James repeated his advice. Wharton listened carefully and decided her new friend was right. She was to keep on listening

Henry James, the great American novelist, was one of Wharton's favorite people. James was also a close friend of Walter Berry, with whom he shared a deep affection for "the lady of Lenox."

to him until the end of his life. (James died in 1916.)

Wharton considered James one of the wisest and kindest men she had ever known. Impressed with Wharton's talent, her elegance, and her unquenchable thirst for new insights into the human condition, James returned her admiration.

In the years to come—some of which would be very dark for Wharton—James would be occasionally alarmed by her passionate intensity, by the explosive energy with which she approached life. He nevertheless remained her steadfast friend, always ready to offer his unconditional support and affection.

James returned the Whartons' visit the following year, arriving at The Mount with Howard Sturgis in October 1904. Along with Walter Berry, also a guest at the time, the visitors and their hosts toured the New England countryside. The American-born James—who had been away from his native land for 20 years—was delighted with the area's "mountain-and-valley, lake-and-river beauty." In the evenings the friends gathered around one of The Mount's many elaborate marble fireplaces and read aloud.

On one such memorable night, James left Wharton spellbound by his "chanting" of poetry by Walt Whitman, whom both considered to be America's greatest poet. Party-loving Teddy Wharton, always eager to please his handsome but puzzling wife, endured these poetry sessions stoically. Although the Whartons were utterly unalike, they were truly fond of one another.

Edith Wharton was 43 years old when she wrote The House of Mirth. *Many critics regard Lily Bart, the heroine of the 1905 novel, as Wharton's most brilliantly etched character.*

FOUR

A Woman in Love

Wharton's expanding social life was matched by her increasing self-confidence. Her days of frequent illness behind her, she worked steadily, writing poems, short stories, and magazine articles. By 1904 she had almost finished another novel. This one would draw, as James had suggested, on Wharton's own experience. *The House of Mirth* was set in the fashionable and wealthy New York of Wharton's youth.

In *The House of Mirth* Wharton illuminated the worst aspects of New York society. She focused on the fears that had most frightened her when she was growing up: imprisonment and isolation. The novel traces the tragic life of Lily Bart, a stylish but impoverished young woman who hopes to succeed in New York society through her beauty and "ornamental" skills.

Bart's sole ambition is to marry a wealthy man who will take care of her for the rest of her life. Summing up her goals, she says simply, "I must have a great deal of money." To obtain it, she grovels before the social leaders of New York society. She works hard for invitations to elegant dinner parties and expensive resorts, and she makes herself available to the richest men she can find.

Society sees Bart as nothing more than a beautiful object. Her tragedy is that she accepts that definition. Serving as a mirror for other people's expectations and desires, she has no sense of herself as an independent woman. Of her heroine, Wharton writes, "She was like some rare flower grown for exhibition, a flower from which every bud had been nipped except the crowning blossom of her beauty. There had never been a time

Wharton used New York City — seen here in 1901 — as the setting for many scenes in The House of Mirth, *her sensitive and sometimes savage portrait of wealthy Americans at the turn of the century.*

when she had any real relation to life."

Bart glimpses a better kind of life, but she is trapped by her own goals. Only one person, a young lawyer named Lawrence Selden, tries to suggest a different path for Bart, but he proves too weak to help her. Worse, even he ends up treating her as a decorative object rather than as a mature woman.

Bart fails to reach her goal. Overwhelmed by frustration and despair, she dies of an overdose of drugs. She has been destroyed by the selfishness and indifference of the very world she tried to enter.

The House of Mirth, published in 1905, was Wharton's first great novel. It quickly became the best-selling book in the United States. Wharton was flooded with letters of congratulation and praise, many from women who identified with Lily Bart. Male readers, too, were moved by the book. Howard Sturgis wrote, "How good! How good!

It is to my mind the best thing you have done. . . . On this one subject (and possibly embroidery) I know what I'm talking about."

The House of Mirth was so successful it hardly needed promotion. Scribners nevertheless advertised the book by claiming that in it, "for the first time the veil has been lifted from New York society."

Wharton was appalled by such hard-sell publicity. With the newfound strength of a best-selling author, she briskly requested Scribners to "stop the spread of that pestilential paragraph." She was, she added, "sick at

Visiting The Mount in 1909, Walter Berry strikes a pose on a terrace wall. Contemporary gossip suggested that he had been the model for Lawrence Selden in The House of Mirth.

Playwright Clyde Fitch dramatized The House of Mirth *in 1906. Although he had authored several hit shows, Fitch failed with this one. "A doleful play," said* The New York Times.

the recollection of it!" The publisher meekly complied.

Popular though it was, *The House of Mirth* received some negative reviews. Wharton was criticized for her choice of "utterly unsuitable" subject matter and for creating characters who lacked virtue.

Wharton had been ecstatic about the glowing reviews of her first book, but by the time *The House of Mirth* was published she was paying little attention to anything—favorable or otherwise—said about her writing. She had developed, as one admiring friend put it, a "fine indifference" to the opinions of others.

Soon after the publication of *The House of Mirth*, the Whartons left for their annual visit to Europe. Most wealthy people of the day traveled extensively as a matter of course, but to Edith Wharton, travel was more than a conventional pastime. She loved to be on the move; it was only then, she once noted, "that I really felt alive."

Automobiles were uncommon at the turn of the century, even among the rich. Edith Wharton, however, had always been interested in the latest technology. (Her house in Lenox had been among the first to have electric lights and a telephone.) She was naturally drawn to "horseless carriages," particularly because they related to one of her favorite activities. "The motor car," she said, "has restored the romance of travel."

The Whartons had bought their first car—a Panhard-Levassor—in Paris in 1904. Edith Wharton, who called the vehicle a "comet," a "magic carpet," a

As well as novels and short stories, Wharton wrote numerous magazine articles. This pencil sketch by artist Kate Rogers Nowell accompanied a travel piece Wharton published in 1906.

A goggled driver demonstrates a Panhard- Levassor touring car. Edith and Teddy Wharton bought the same model — which she called a "magic carpet" — in Paris in 1904.

"chariot"—anything but the spluttering, unpredictable device it was—adored it. The car meant freedom. In it she could go anywhere she wanted, escaping the bondage of fixed hours and the beaten path.

Over the years, Wharton would own a parade of shiny new cars. "One visualizes her," writes one of her biographers, R. W. B. Lewis, "sitting bolt upright in the high front seat of the Panhard, unprotected by windshield, side doors, or hood; Teddy beside her at the wheel, wearing goggles and a canvas coat; she herself veiled and swathed from head to foot in a long dust-covered cape, chiffon scarf flying about her hair, her hands clutching her head."

During the Whartons' 1906 European trip, they motored through parts of France they had never seen. Edith Wharton was enchanted by the medieval castles and cathedrals, by the monuments built by Roman invaders centuries earlier, by the abundant or-

Chauffeur Charles Cook, pictured with one of Wharton's cars in Paris, worked for the author for 17 years. He drove her through New England, North Africa, and much of Europe.

The velvety lawns and splashing fountains of Wharton's garden at The Mount formed an elegant backdrop for literary conversation when Morton Fullerton visited her in 1907.

chards and wooded hillsides through which she "flew" in her "chariot."

Eager to share such wonders, she invited her dear friend Henry James to come along for a similar tour the following year. The conservative James was reluctant to commit himself to a long trip in a newfangled motorcar, but after he had finally agreed, he enjoyed himself thoroughly. "Never was there a more delightful traveling companion," wrote Wharton. James, she said, was "never bored, never disappointed and never . . . missing any of the little fine touches of sensation that enrich the movements of the really good traveler."

The drives through the French countryside inspired Wharton to write a series of enthusiastic travel pieces for the *Atlantic Monthly* magazine. In 1908 these articles were published as *A Motor-Flight Through France*, considered by many critics the best of Wharton's numerous travel books.

Although the Whartons were fond of each other, their marriage was more like a business partnership than a love match. Teddy Wharton, who had long since spent his own inheritance, contributed to the couple's economy by managing his wife's money. His favorite occupations were fishing, hunting, and horseback riding; he read almost nothing—not even his wife's work—and he was thoroughly bored by the conversation of her intellectual circle. He was,

he once admitted to a friend, "no good on 'Puss's' [Edith Wharton's family nickname] high plain of thought."

After 22 years of marriage, Edith Wharton had almost resigned herself to a life without romantic love. When she was 45 years old, however, she met a man who sent a shock wave through her existence. He was Morton Fullerton, a 42-year-old American journalist.

The son of a clergyman, Fullerton had grown up in Waltham, Massachusetts. He had graduated from Harvard with literary honors and moved to England, where he took a job with the London *Times*. In England he met Henry James, who was much impressed with the promising young man. The two became good friends; when Fullerton was transferred to Paris by the *Times*, he continued his friendship with James through regular correspondence.

Edith and Teddy Wharton led a busy social life during their stays in Paris. In the spring of 1907 they often crossed paths with Fullerton, a witty and popular member of Paris society. He soon became a frequent dinner guest at the Whartons' elegant rented apartment. Fullerton was single, although he had once been married briefly to a young Frenchwoman. Well-built and good-looking, he was said by knowledgeable Parisians to have had numerous love affairs.

When Fullerton wrote Henry James

that he planned a trip to the United States, the novelist urged him to visit Lenox, Massachusetts, where their mutual friends, Edith and Teddy Wharton, were back in residence. Fullerton arrived at The Mount in the fall of 1907.

Edith Wharton knew nothing of Fullerton's romantic past. What she saw was a charming and attractive intellectual whose passions were for literature and art—a man totally unlike her husband. When her visitor revealed that he was writing an essay on Henry James's fiction, she was intrigued. The two spent hours discussing their friend's work.

The first snowfall of the year began on the second day of Fullerton's visit. He and Wharton took a walk in the woods, where they found a witch hazel bush, its fragile yellow flowers blooming above the powdery snow. Smiling in delight, each picked a sprig. When Fullerton left The Mount a few days later, he enclosed his flower between the pages of an intimate note of appreciation to Wharton.

Soon after Fullerton returned to Paris, Wharton began to keep a secret journal (discovered in her papers after her death). In it, she wrote as though she were addressing Fullerton. "Finding myself—after so long!—with someone to talk to, I take up this empty volume," reads the first entry. "Now I shall have the illusion that I am talking

American journalist Morton Fullerton writes a letter in the library of his Paris apartment. The dashing correspondent, who met Wharton when she was 45 years old, was the great love of her life.

to you, and that—as when I picked the witch hazel—something of what I say will somehow reach you."

The Whartons normally left for their European visit in January; after Fullerton's visit, Edith Wharton decided to leave in early December. She had already come to think of Paris as the center of her social and intellectual life; with Fullerton there, it soon became the heart of her emotional existence as well.

Wharton's latest novel, *The Fruit of the Tree*, had been published just before she left for Paris. Dealing with mercy killing and the working conditions of mill laborers, it had not sold quite as well as its predecessor, *The House of Mirth*, but it was nevertheless a critical and financial success.

As soon as the Whartons arrived in the French capital, they were pulled into its social whirl. They dined out almost every night and frequently attended the Paris "salons"—gatherings where the brightest and most famous people in Europe met to talk about every facet of the human experience, from art to philosophy to politics. Among the most popular topics were Wharton's new book and *The House of Mirth*, which had just appeared in a French-language edition.

Edith Wharton was in her element at the Paris salons—and so was the popular Fullerton, who was invited everywhere. He often escorted Edith Wharton to concerts, lectures, and plays that held no interest for her husband.

Although Wharton was finding little time to write, she had never been happier. Showing no outward sign of the way she felt, she continued to write in her secret journal, still addressing her words to an unaware Fullerton. "The other night at the theater, when you came into the box," she wrote in February 1908, "I felt for the first time that indescribable current of communication flowing between myself and someone else . . . and said to myself, 'This must be what happy women feel.' "

Teddy Wharton, who had never shared his wife's enjoyment of the kind of life they were now living, was restless and bored. He soon began to complain of severe headaches. Although he and his wife were not scheduled to return to Massachusetts until May, he sailed for home in March, planning to take a "cure" at a fashionable health resort in Arkansas.

Edith Wharton genuinely cared for her husband, and she was worried about his health. She was also delighted by the chance to spend more time alone with Fullerton. The two strolled through the flower-filled parks of Paris, went for drives in the country, visited old churches and castles. It was spring, it was Paris. Edith Wharton, for the first time in her life, was in love.

After Wharton began her love affair

Everyday sights in the French countryside took on a new beauty for Wharton when she saw them in the company of Morton Fullerton in the spring of 1908.

with Fullerton, time seemed to be passing more swiftly than ever before. "In another month," she wrote in April, "I shall be gone, I shan't see you, I shan't hear your voice.... All I want is to be near you, to feel my hands in yours. Ah, if you ever read these lines, you will know you have been loved!"

In spite of her obsession with Fullerton, Wharton continued to act the role of a socially correct member of society. No one—except Henry James, the good friend of both lovers—suspected that her relationship with Ful-

lerton was more complex than it appeared on the surface.

Wharton's joy in her love for Fullerton was tempered by her feelings of guilt. Her ethical concepts were strong: had she the right, she asked herself, to violate traditional standards of conduct? Did any married woman—no matter how unhappy her marriage— have the right to have an affair? Did she have the right to risk causing pain to the man she had married?

Wharton's dilemma was resolved by a combination of choice, circumstance,

Notre Dame Cathedral towers over Paris, the city where Wharton fell in love with Fullerton. She ended their romance in 1910, but she remained his friend for the rest of her life.

and the passage of time. Following her long-established travel schedule, she returned to the United States in May 1908. The departure was agonizing.

"How the witch hazel has kept its promise since it flowered in our hands last October!" she wrote Fullerton from shipboard. "Bring me, magic flower, one more day such as those—but dearer, nearer, by all these death-pangs of separation with which my heart is torn."

Coming home was not easy. Teddy Wharton met his wife in New York; the two then boarded the train to Massachusetts. Edith Wharton wrote about the trip in her secret journal. Excited by a new book about heredity that she was reading, she passed it on to her husband. "The answer," wrote Edith Wharton, "was 'Does that sort of thing really amuse you?' I heard the key turn in my prison-lock. That is the answer to everything worthwhile! Oh, Gods of derision! And you've given me over 20 years of it!"

At The Mount, Wharton did her best to work and to act like her usual self.

Her efforts were successful. In September 1908 she published *The Hermit and the Wild Woman*, her fourth collection of short stories. She wrote several magazine articles and worked on her new novel, which would be called *The Custom of the Country*.

The Whartons returned to Europe in the fall of 1908, repeating much of the previous year's pattern. The following spring, after Teddy Wharton once more returned to America alone, Edith Wharton and Morton Fullerton went to England to visit their friend Henry James.

By now, a small circle of friends, including James and Howard Sturgis, knew about the Wharton-Fullerton relationship. Aware of the realities of Wharton's long, sad marriage, these friends were sympathetic and supportive. Before the couple left for a motor tour of England with James, Sturgis wrote Wharton a note. "Keep it up—run your race," he said, "fly your flight—live your romances—drain the cup of pleasure to the dregs."

The "race," however, was almost run. Fullerton, never a man to endure prolonged separation from the opposite sex, had renewed an old romance in the time he had been separated from Wharton. Always a candid man, he told Wharton about his divided loyalty. He also indirectly asked Wharton for money to buy back a set of incriminating letters with which another former lover was blackmailing him. (A Wharton short story, "The Letters," is based on this incident.)

Wharton's journal does not explain the precise reason for the end of her romance, but the reappearance of Fullerton's old lover and his use of Wharton's money to pay his blackmailer probably affected it strongly. In any case, by 1910 her infatuation with the magnetic Fullerton had cooled.

Whatever else he had been, Fullerton had also been Wharton's friend, and she took friendship very seriously. She kept in touch with him, by visits and letters, until the end of her life. (Four years younger than Wharton, Fullerton outlived her by 15 years. He died at the age of 86 in 1952.)

Edith Wharton had always considered divorce unthinkable, but her husband's mental and emotional instability finally led her to end her 28-year marriage in 1913.

FIVE

"America's Best Living Novelist"

Edith Wharton had never been happy in her marriage, but she had never considered leaving Teddy Wharton, even when she was in love with Morton Fullerton. A few years after the end of that love affair, however, the Wharton marriage fell apart.

When Teddy Wharton married Edith Jones in 1885, he had been physically robust, an avid sportsman and traveler. His health had remained excellent for the next 20 years, but by 1908 it was deteriorating seriously. He had begun to suffer from mysterious headaches and to experience severe pains in his arms and legs. He had also become mentally unpredictable.

As his wife's literary reputation soared, Teddy Wharton's spirits sank. He began to have extreme mood swings, from deep depression to extreme exhilaration. He had been hospitalized several times after his trip to the health resort in Arkansas in 1908.

Teddy Wharton had no vocation, no interest in his wife's social or intellectual life, and no physical relationship with her. After his own inheritance had dwindled away to nothing, he had become financially dependent on her. He had started to see himself as irrelevant and powerless. Edith Wharton had tried to improve this view by putting him in charge of her estate.

In 1909 Teddy Wharton made an astonishing confession to his wife. He told her he had sold a large number of her stocks and bought an apartment in Boston, where he had been living with another woman. After she recovered from her amazement at this news from her spouse, Edith Wharton agreed to

Teddy Wharton, once an adoring husband, had become increasingly hostile toward his wife, but he never understood why she divorced him. "Puss shouldn't have done that to me," he said.

"forget" the matter; her husband's mother had recently died, and he replaced the misappropriated funds from his inheritance.

After a period of extended travel, Teddy Wharton's physical health improved, but he remained a deeply unhappy man. His wife refused to let him resume his management of her financial affairs; without that occupation he had nothing to do. By 1911 he was staging regular scenes, alternating between angry demands that he be allowed to resume control of his wife's financial affairs and tearful admissions that he was too ill to do so.

Many of Teddy Wharton's scenes with his wife occurred in front of friends and guests, including Henry James. After a particularly violent confrontation at The Mount in the summer of 1911, James observed to a friend, "The violent and scenic Teddy is negotiable in a measure—but the pleading, suffering, clinging, helpless Teddy is a very awful ... quantity indeed."

Edith Wharton had taken to spending almost all her time abroad. When she received a handsome offer for The Mount in 1911, she began to think about selling the property. Her husband had announced that unless she allowed him to run the estate he would not live with her there. She began to consider a formal separation from him.

In the midst of all the domestic upheaval, Edith Wharton doggedly continued to write. In September 1911 she published *Ethan Frome*, a short novel considered by some critics to be her masterpiece. Woven into the book were some of her most deeply felt personal emotions.

Ethan Frome is a New England farmer married to Zenobia, an older woman who complains constantly about her health and who belittles her husband every chance she gets. Working for the couple is Zenobia's cousin, Mattie Silver, a lively and charming young woman closer in age to Ethan than to his wife.

Mattie and Ethan fall in love, but believing their future hopeless they resolve to commit suicide. Their effort to die in a crash on a snowy hillside results in a bizarre tragedy. Both survive, but Mattie is crippled for life. The two continue to live in misery with Zenobia.

The parallels between *Ethan Frome* and Edith Wharton's own life are clear. Ethan's wife—like Wharton's husband—is older, extremely neurotic, and totally absorbed in her own health. Mattie Silver—like Morton Fullerton—is young, sympathetic, and sensitive. She shares Ethan's interests, just as Fullerton shared Wharton's. Zenobia and Ethan's quarrels echo the verbal battles that had become a regular part of the Whartons' relationship with each other.

The conclusion of *Ethan Frome*—in

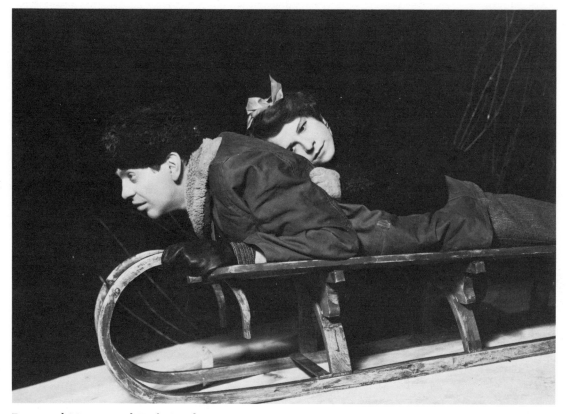

Raymond Massey and Ruth Gordon prepare to enact the suicide-attempt scene in the 1936 dramatization of Wharton's celebrated 1911 novel, Ethan Frome.

which the life-affirming lovers are both destroyed by the spite of the grim and twisted Zenobia—illustrates Edith Wharton's nightmarish projection of her own existence. When the book was published it was widely praised, although many critics objected to its uncompromisingly stark view of life. It nevertheless became a classic and is today the most frequently read of all Wharton's books.

After selling The Mount in 1912,

Edith Wharton moved to Europe; although she would return to the United States on visits, she would make her life abroad from this point on. She never, however, stopped thinking of herself as an American. Teddy Wharton remained for a while in Boston; when he came to Europe he refused to see his wife, clearly preferring the company of the many different women he escorted publicly.

Divorce had become commonplace

While Wharton did not share her mother's passion for clothes, she always dressed well. She often wore low-cut gowns to emphasize her figure, which remained trim well into her middle years.

Caught unaware by a camera-carrying fellow guest, Wharton puffs away at a French garden party. Few American women smoked in public before the 1920s, but the habit was accepted in France.

among the wealthy of the time, but to 51-year-old Edith Wharton, it still seemed disgraceful. People like herself, she felt, did not divorce. Only the "new rich"—those materialistic individuals who had begun to find their place in society in the late 19th century—practiced divorce with almost no moral reservations.

Most of Wharton's friends and rela-tives, however, were urging her to sever her relationship with Teddy Wharton. The people closest to her, she wrote to a friend, "have been writing me on all sides that I must 'act'; so I hope some-thing may soon be decently, silently, and soberly arranged."

As she was painfully contemplating her own divorce, Wharton was finish-ing *The Custom of the Country*, a great novel that laid bare the moral emptiness of the "new rich." In this book she contrasted the representatives of "old" New York—honorable and committed to tradition—with the pleasure-seeking, amoral members of New York's "modern" society.

The central character of *The Custom of the Country* is Undine Spragg, a beautiful but greedy young woman from a newly wealthy Midwestern family. Spragg, whose selfish desires know no limit, marries and divorces again and again in her quest for power and fortune.

Like the ambitious heroines of many other Wharton novels, Spragg is forced to use her beauty to achieve her goals. Unlike others—particularly Lily Bart in *The House of Mirth*—Spragg is victorious at the end of the novel. She has trampled on the lives of those who trusted her, but she has conquered her world.

Published in 1913, *The Custom of the Country* pleased both reviewers and readers. As had happened before, Wharton was criticized for her cool, unsentimental characterizations—Undine Spragg was called "the most disagreeable girl in American fiction"—but the book sold thousands of copies and confirmed Wharton's place as America's best living novelist.

In April 1913 Edith Wharton was granted a divorce by a Paris judge. It had been the most agonizing move of

Wharton, who — like most women of her era and social class — rode sidesaddle, prepares for an early-morning jaunt. An enthusiastic and skillful rider, she stabled 14 horses at The Mount.

her life. She and Teddy Wharton had been married for 28 years.

Wharton had been tormented and guilt-ridden about getting her divorce; after it, she felt free for the first time in her life. She spent the next year in travel, often accompanied by Walter Berry, her old friend and frequent companion over the years.

Berry, once a potential suitor of Wharton, had remained—and would continue to be—a bachelor. Friends speculated that the pair might marry;

A vast and silent fortress looms over the sands of Tunisia, one of the countries Wharton visited in 1914. Awed and delighted by the desert, she returned to North Africa three years later.

however, they were actually more like brother and sister than lovers.

After visits to Italy, England, Germany, and the United States, Wharton decided to tour North Africa. Because Walter Berry was in India at the time, she invited another friend, Percy Lubbock, to join her.

Lubbock, a young English writer who, more than 30 years later, would write a biography called *Portrait of Edith Wharton*, accepted with delight. In early 1914, the pair sailed from France for Algeria, accompanied by Wharton's secretary, personal maid, chauffeur, and large touring car.

To travelers in the early part of the 20th century, Africa symbolized the unknown, the mysterious. This was exactly why Wharton had chosen it for her destination. Still recovering from the shock of her divorce, she wanted to find, as she told a friend, a world "far from everything I know." The trip supplied what she was looking for.

Accustomed to the clutter and racket of cities, she was enchanted by the immensity of the empty desert and

Merchants show their wares in a North African bazaar, a sight that intrigued Wharton. Such scenes, she said, made her feel she had discovered a "page of the Arabian Nights."

its eerie silences. "I had no idea," she wrote, "what desert magic could be." Everything in North Africa was new and strange to Wharton and Lubbock, and everything fascinated them. Driving through Algeria and Tunisia, they visited shadowy ruins, desert oases, exotic bazaars.

One event of the trip, however, was less than "magic." Waking up one night in a remote Algerian inn, Wharton reached for a light and found herself touching a strange hand. She leaped out of bed and ran for the door. It re-fused to budge. The intruder grabbed her, but she struggled free and tugged at the door. It finally opened, releasing a screaming Wharton into the hallway.

By the time the rest of Wharton's party arrived, the uninvited guest had escaped. Assuring Lubbock that she was unharmed, Wharton then calmly returned to her bed. The next morning, her curiosity and enthusiasm undampened, she led the way to the car for further exploration. Lubbock was impressed. "Her gallantry," he later told a mutual friend, "has been amazing."

Wharton shows off three of her Pekinese, the breed of dog she liked best. Firmly convinced that they had souls, Wharton treated her pets more like children than animals.

S I X

War

On June 28, 1914, shots rang out in Sarajevo, the capital of the Austrian-occupied province of Bosnia (now part of Yugoslavia). Archduke Franz Ferdinand, heir to the throne of Austria-Hungary, had been killed.

To Wharton, newly returned from North Africa, and her friends, the assassination seemed a dim and distant episode. It was, however, the first event in what would be the most ferocious conflict the planet had ever known. World War I had begun.

Austria-Hungary, declaring the archduke's murder to be the work of its neighbor, Serbia, promptly declared war on that small nation. The next day, Russian troops massed at the Austrian border, and within a week, all the major nations of Europe were at war.

On one side were the Central Powers—Germany, Austria-Hungary, Turkey, and Bulgaria. Opposing them were the Allies—Russia, France, England, and Japan. Italy joined the Allies in 1915, the United States in 1917.

Strange as it seems today, the war's participants entered the conflict with excitement, even jubilation. Citizens of all the involved countries believed that the war would be brief, the sacrifices small, the victory easily won. They were, of course, terribly wrong.

The "Great War," as it was known at the time, would drag on for four murderous years. It brought with it new techniques in mass destruction: poison gas was introduced, as were armored tanks, airplanes, barbed wire, and submarines.

The main attacks on Germany took place along the western front, a line stretching from the coast of Belgium to Verdun, a town in northeastern France.

Allied soldiers advance along the western front in 1914. Although the weapons used in World War I were primitive by today's standards, the war's casualty rate was one of history's highest.

Both sides dug elaborate systems of defensive trenches along this front. For most of the war's duration, advances or retreats along this trench line were limited to a few miles, often even a few yards.

The casualties of the war were staggering. In one battle, on the Somme River in France, more than one million French, British, and German soldiers were killed or wounded. Nor was the savagery of World War I limited to the battlefield. Along with the 10 million soldiers of both sides who lost their lives, some 12 million civilians were wounded or killed, and many more were made homeless.

Wharton had enjoyed the summer of 1914. Rumors of war had been circulating, but few people in Paris took them seriously. The city, bursting with exciting cultural activity, had never been more splendid.

The great modern dancer, Isadora

Duncan, was performing at the Paris Opera, dazzling audiences with her new, free style. She danced, observed Wharton in her journal, the way she herself would if she knew how—with graceful abandon and flowing, uninhibited movement. The celebrated Russian Ballet was also in town. Extraordinary works were being produced by such writers as Marcel Proust and Jean Cocteau.

Even after France entered the war, on August 3, there were few signs of concern in Paris. Like most of the people she knew, Wharton thought the war would be over in a matter of weeks. Not even Henry James's gloomy prediction—that the war would bring about "the crash of civilization"—dispelled Wharton's feelings of optimism.

Since 1909 Wharton had kept a beautiful apartment in Paris on the Rue de Varenne, in the heart of the city's wealthiest and most aristocratic section, the Faubourg St. Germain. Nearby were some of the city's most exciting salons, where she continued to mingle with diplomats and men and women of letters.

One of these salons, however, was apparently not to Wharton's taste. This one was conducted by Gertrude Stein, another American expatriate (a person who chooses to live away from his or her native country).

Stein's group at one time or another included novelists Ernest Hemingway

Isadora Duncan performs in "Aulis," one of the unconventional pieces for which she was celebrated. The American dancer and her troupe were wildly popular in prewar Paris.

and James Joyce and artist Pablo Picasso. Wharton frequently entertained such eminent writers as André Gide, Paul Valéry and, later, Sinclair Lewis and Aldous Huxley. Curiously, the creative people who centered themselves around Wharton had almost no con-

American author Gertrude Stein — perhaps most famous for her line, "A rose is a rose is a rose" — presided over a Paris salon of creative people that included Ernest Hemingway and James Joyce.

tact with those who met regularly with Stein.

Wharton felt completely at home in France. She considered the French to be a wonderfully honest people, facing the facts of life without fear or prudery. They respected the past, and they honored art, literature, and beauty—to Wharton, the most important elements of life. Furthermore, the French, she insisted, loved ideas more than money.

As the war progressed, Wharton began to see that France itself—along with everything she valued most—was

threatened. She watched in horror as the Germans swept through neighboring Belgium, systematically laying waste to the countryside and its population. She was shocked when the German army burned the medieval city of Louvain, site of a famous library full of rare and irreplaceable books, and when they bombarded the city of Rheims and its towering cathedral.

Paris was suddenly numb and silent. Shops were closed, windows boarded up, streets deserted. The city was as silent as the North African desert. The war was coming closer; major battles were being fought only 50 miles away. Paris was under martial (military) law. By the end of August 1914, 140,000 French soldiers had been killed or wounded, and one million German soldiers were on French soil.

One of the war's earliest and most important confrontations was the Battle of the Marne, waged in mid-September along the Marne River, a few miles from Paris. The German army finally retreated, thanks very largely to 6,000 French troops who had been sent racing to the fight in 600 Parisian taxicabs. Another major battle took place in Ypres, some hundred miles north of Paris, between October 12 and November 11.

Refugees from these two battles began to pour into Paris. Most were simple country people; many of them were children; some, from areas near the

Smoke pours from Rheims Cathedral following a 1914 German raid. Heavily damaged, the 13th-century French church was rebuilt after the war by American millionaire John D. Rockefeller.

French youngsters comfort one another amid the ruins of their homes. Children, always among the first victims of war, made up a large part of the swelling tide of refugees in 1914.

Belgian-French border, could speak no French. All of them were homeless, penniless, and hungry. And all were in a state of shock after seeing the devastation inflicted on their homes and communities.

Ever since her childhood, Wharton had felt deep compassion for all living things, particularly for those who suffered unjustly. Many of her wealthy acquaintances were content to wait in comfort until the war ended, but she yearned to be of some use. As a woman, she could not serve on the front lines. She could, however, do her best to help these crowds of helpless and desper-

ate people, victims of what she called the "shrieking fury" of the times.

A new Edith Wharton was born during World War I. A shy, lonely child, she had grown up to be a self-reliant but depressed young society matron. Then she had revealed herself as a richly gifted writer and a sophisticated and constant traveler. Now she was a humanitarian, equipped with almost demonic energy and a superb talent for organization.

In the fall of 1914 Wharton set about establishing the American Hostels for Refugees, a system of shelters for those made homeless by the war. Begging

Homeless after the ferocious battle of Ypres, dazed French villagers set out in search of shelter. The roads to Paris were clogged with such forlorn groups in 1914.

and borrowing, she acquired the use of several large houses in Paris; into them, she placed hundreds of displaced families.

Next, she organized kitchens, which distributed meals to 600 people a day. She also set up and operated a clinic staffed by doctors and nurses who gave free medical services to the many invalids among the refugees. Most of the people straggling into Paris were in rags; Wharton organized collections of clothing and shoes from France and the United States and oversaw their distribution.

She also opened an employment agency, helping hundreds of people find work; to those waiting for employment, she supplied cash. Wharton's herculean efforts were funded partly from her own purse, partly by money she raised from friends and acquaintances. In the first year of her humanitarian mission, she raised more than $100,000, a respectable business achievement for a woman who had never had to work for her living.

At the end of 1915 Wharton added up the year's results. Her organization had helped 9,330 refugees, served

235,000 meals, and distributed 48,000 articles of clothing. Medical care had been given to 7,700 people, jobs located for 3,400.

Assisting Wharton in her refugee program were a number of what she called "good angels." They included such new acquaintances as the writer André Gide and such longtime friends as Walter Berry. The people who knew her best were awed by Wharton's accomplishments. "All the Belgians in Paris," said Berry to a friend, "are feeding out of Edith's hands."

Wharton's work was appreciated and praised by friends and strangers, by government officials and refugees. She appeared to take both the work and the praise casually. She showed none of the smug and patronizing attitude so often displayed by women of her social position who engaged in "charity."

One friend noted that Wharton "speaks less of her good works than anyone I know." And when people expressed admiration, said the friend, Wharton turned them off "laughingly." Percy Lubbock, the writer with whom she had toured North Africa, jokingly said he had nothing against her whirlwind activities because she clearly did not enjoy them. He undoubtedly suspected that she had never done anything that gratified her so much.

Wharton, who always remained an American citizen, strongly believed

Their men in the army, their livestock killed by German soldiers, French farm women hitch themselves to a plow. Much of the French countryside faced acute food shortages during World War I.

that the United States should join the Allies in their effort to defeat Germany. Already doing the work of several people, she began to write a stream of articles for American newspapers and magazines, reporting on conditions in Europe and appealing vigorously for a U.S. declaration of war.

In February 1915 Wharton and Walter Berry volunteered to deliver medical supplies to field hospitals on the front lines. The war's destruction was evident within a few miles of Paris. There were shell-shocked soldiers, ruined and empty farmhouses, and ambulances carrying wounded men away from the battlefront.

On their way to the military hospitals

A lone military officer surveys a ravaged country road in 1914. The savage battles of World War I produced similar eerie and desolate landscapes across much of France.

in the town of Verdun, Wharton and Berry found themselves within a few miles of a battle. Peering across a valley with binoculars, they could see a pattern of trenches, a grim landscape dotted with knots of advancing soldiers and puffs of smoke from artillery. Even from a distance, the roar of the cannonading was deafening. Finding it hard to believe they had witnessed war with their own eyes, the two friends

drove in silence to Verdun, where they delivered their much-needed cargo.

During the next few months Wharton visited battle areas again and again. She became a kind of war correspondent, sending her firsthand reports back to the United States. Americans, to whom the war in far-off Europe still seemed unreal, learned much of war from her dispatches.

Wharton wrote of scenes like the one at the front lines in southern France, where she sensed "the invisible power of evil, a saturation of the whole landscape with some hidden vitriol of hate." She wrote of the day when she accidentally wandered to the edge of a line of German trenches. She had been led away by a young French lieutenant who took her through a dark tunnel to a gutted farmhouse that served as a headquarters for a French army unit.

Among the war's casualties were innumerable buildings ranging from simple farmhouses to cathedrals. Wharton was moved by the sight of the ruined structures in France. She had always thought of buildings almost as living things, associating houses with people, people with houses.

She grieved when she saw the damage wrought by the Germans on the great cathedral at Rheims: one of Europe's most magnificent buildings, she wrote, had been struck by "death and disease." Even more poignant to Whar-

Overseen by a statue of the Virgin Mary, refugee children assemble outside the Children of Flanders Rescue Center, one of the shelters organized by Edith Wharton during World War I.

ton were the shattered homes of ordinary people, so many of which, she observed sadly, had been "bombarded to death."

As in all wars, many of those who suffered the most during World War I were children. Thousands of boys and girls had been left homeless as a result of the battles fought in Belgium. Many had been found in burned-out houses, alone and hungry after the deaths of their parents.

In the summer of 1915, a year after the start of the war, Wharton received a telegram from the Belgian government. Aware of her tireless efforts to help refugees, the Belgians asked if she would be willing to take charge of a group of 60 Belgian children who were about to arrive in Paris. Wharton never even considered saying no.

By the time the orphaned children, weary, dirty, and frightened, arrived in Paris two days later, Wharton had obtained the use of an old schoolhouse in the city. Here she fed the youngsters, gave them clean clothing and warm beds. By the end of the year she and her assistants were operating six residences and taking care of 750 children.

Wharton, who had never been cold or hungry herself, was deeply moved

Two of Wharton's "good angels" survey the girls' dormitory at the St. Ouen refugee shelter near Paris. The neatly hung hats were among the articles of clothing provided by Wharton's committee.

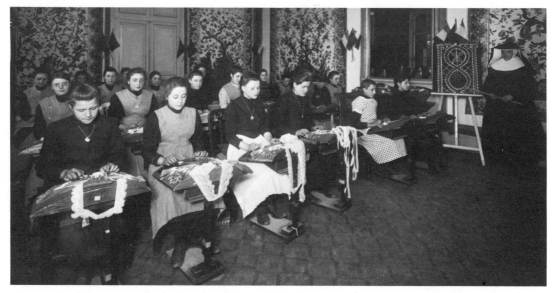

Teenage refugees attend a lacemaking class at the St. Ouen shelter. Concerned about the young people's futures, Wharton insisted that they be educated as well as clothed and fed.

by the sight of the forlorn children pouring into Paris. Her work with them was one of her life's greatest satisfactions. She would never forget the day when 90 little boys arrived at one of her shelters. Shy and fearful at first, their faces brightened when they saw the welcoming smiles of Wharton and her friends. As they marched into their new home, the boys began to sing the Belgian national anthem.

There seemed to be no limit to Wharton's energy and eagerness to help others during the chaotic days of 1915. Her friends were impressed with her work, but many of them thought that, at the age of 54, she was stretching herself to the breaking point. They urged her to slow down, but she told them she would not consider it. There were too many people who needed her. Besides, her work gave her less time to think about the horrors of the war. "The sadness of all things is beyond words," she wrote to a friend, "and hard work is the only escape from it."

Few weeks passed in which Wharton did not hear about the loss of good friends on the battlefield. "My heart is heavy," she wrote, "with the sorrow of all my friends who are in mourning."

February 1916 brought more heartbreaking news, this time from England: Henry James was dead of a stroke at the age of 73. A sympathetic and generous friend as well as an invaluable literary adviser, James had meant more

The remains of a German soldier, discovered two months after his death in battle, give mute testimony to the carnage of World War I. By the end of the conflict, 10 million men had died.

to Wharton than almost anyone she had ever known. "His friendship," she said later, "was the pride and honor of my life."

The government of France was impressed with Wharton's herculean efforts. In April 1916 the nation's president awarded her the Cross of the Legion of Honor, France's highest decoration. As well as appreciating Wharton's aid to the refugees, the French much admired the modesty of the woman they called "our noble American friend."

Wharton's "enormous and varied work," said an editorial in the newspaper *Le Figaro*, "is a silent work; this energy, this apostle's faith are hidden beneath an air . . . of having really nothing to do in life and no other concern except to observe approvingly the good things being done by other people." Another newspaper observed that Wharton "does good works without seeming to notice it."

Still immersed in her "good works," Wharton began a new book, *Summer*, in 1916. A short but powerful novel, *Summer* is set in an isolated village in the Berkshire Hills, the same area Wharton had chosen for *Ethan Frome*. The story's central character, an intense young woman named Charity Royall, is abandoned by her family, a group of drunken outlaws who live in a desolate region known as the Mountain. She is rescued by Lawyer Royall, a sometimes harsh but basically decent older man who takes her home and becomes her guardian.

Charity leads a quiet life as the village librarian, but she yearns for romance and excitement. She becomes pregnant by a charming but unreliable artist who briefly stays in the village. Her hopes for marriage are dashed when the young man leaves for a short trip and never returns.

Desperate, Charity returns to the Mountain, the dark and chaotic world where she was born and where she now expects to give birth and die. Once again, however, Lawyer Royall saves her. He brings her back to the village and quietly marries her.

Published in 1917, *Summer* was—as was by now customary—attacked by some reviewers for its "sordid" theme. It was highly praised by most critics and by loyal old friends like Howard Sturgis, who called it a "little gem and wonder."

Summer is a dark and haunting tale. Although it is set in the United States, its brooding, violent atmosphere reflects Wharton's view of "the convulsed" world of wartime. Like many others in Europe, Wharton was beginning to feel that the war, whose fury was steadily increasing, would never end. In April 1917, however, new hope was born: the United States joined the Allied forces.

American soldiers marched into Paris on the Fourth of July, 1917. Parisians shouted their delight, which Wharton shared. She had been urging her country to join the war since it began; the appearance of "our wonderful, incredible troops" after so many months of Europe's agony was, she said, "really splendid."

Sixteen months later Wharton was talking to friends in her apartment when she heard the bells of a nearby church begin to ring. Then bells began to sound from the steeples of other churches; soon the air of Paris was filled with a spectacular, booming chorus of chimes.

Wharton and her friends ran to the balcony of the apartment, not daring

American infantrymen in France react to the news of November 11, 1918: a treaty ending hostilities between Germany and the Allies has just been signed. The Great War is over at last.

to believe what the sounds meant. "We had fared so long on the thin diet of hope deferred," she wrote later, "that for a moment or two our hearts wavered and doubted. Then, like the bells, they swelled to bursting, and we knew the war was over." It was November 11, 1918. Germany had surrendered at last.

Edith Wharton's face expresses pride and pleasure as she receives a Doctor of Letters degree from Yale University in 1923. She was the first woman so honored by the venerable institution.

SEVEN

"An Incorrigible Life-lover"

The war's end left Wharton both exhilarated and reeling with fatigue. She was also burdened with a sense of irretrievable loss. So many had died. Henry James was gone, and by early 1920 so was Wharton's dear old friend Howard Sturgis. He had been, wrote Percy Lubbock, "quick as a flash in wit and ironic intelligence, patient and scrupulous in kindness." His death, said a grieving Wharton, left the world "greatly impoverished."

That world had undergone radical changes since the outset of the war in 1914. Wharton had once thought of Paris as the most civilized and delightful place on earth; now she was tired of it. It had become, as she said in a letter to a friend, "simply awful—a kind of continuous earthquake of motors, buses, trams, lorries, taxis, and other howling and swooping and colliding engines, with hundreds of thousands of U.S. citizens rushing about in them."

Wharton's income had been drastically reduced by her enormous expenditures on relief work during the war and by the newly imposed U.S. income tax. Nevertheless, she was receiving handsome royalties for her books, and her investments continued to provide her with a substantial income. Deciding to move out of Paris in 1919, she bought two houses—the first she had owned since The Mount.

One was Pavillon Colombe, a small estate 12 miles outside Paris. Complete with a pool filled with goldfish and beautiful grounds planted with ancient pear and apple trees, the place suited Wharton perfectly. Here she could write and tend her garden in peace and still have easy access to Paris.

Wharton's other purchase was a

Driven by her smartly uniformed coachman, a 19th-century Parisienne serenely contemplates her handsome city. Gone forever after World War I, this was the Paris that Wharton had loved.

winter home on the French Riviera, at the edge of the Mediterranean Sea. Known as Ste. Claire, the house had once served as a convent. It had a magnificent view of mountains and sea, but it had been unoccupied and neglected for many years. Wharton, who loved to work on old houses, immediately began to remodel and repair it.

Ste. Claire offered Wharton two things she much wanted: a beautiful place to entertain her old friends and a tranquil spot in which to write. Her energy and spirits, at low ebb since the war, returned in full force. "I am thrilled to the spine," she wrote to a friend about Ste. Claire, "and I feel as if I were going to get married—to the right man at last!"

Wharton worked every morning, sit-

Buses, trucks, and automobiles honk and screech their way through the once tranquil Place de l'Opera in Paris. Wharton found the crowded, noisy postwar city "simply awful."

Wharton gazes over the manicured lawns of Pavillon Colombe in 1933. She had purchased the estate, which was just outside Paris, in 1919.

ting up in bed at her writing board, the sparkling Mediterranean visible from her window. She soon began to write *The Age of Innocence*, one of her best novels. Before she had put a word of the book on paper, magazine serialization as well as hardcover publishing rights had been snapped up for more than $30,000, a huge sum for the time.

Wharton set *The Age of Innocence* in the world in which she had grown up—New York in the 1870s. At the time, she had bitterly resented most of what that world had represented, but looking back at it decades later, she saw it in a different light.

She was still critical of the stuffy, narrow attitudes held by the people she knew in her youth, but their world seemed decent and honorable in comparison to the agitated, money-conscious postwar society she saw now.

Ste. Claire, Wharton's winter residence, overlooks both the mountains of southern France and the Mediterranean Sea. It was here that she began to write The Age of Innocence.

"I am steeping myself in the 19th century," she wrote a friend, "which is such a blessed refuge from the turmoil and mediocrity of today—like seeking refuge in a mighty temple."

Wharton peopled *The Age of Innocence* with real individuals she had once known. Notable among them is the hero's mother-in-law; Mrs. Welland is unmistakably a fictionalized version of Wharton's mother, Lucretia Jones.

Most of the novel's other characters—the stern and aristocratic older women, the straitlaced and prim younger women, the handsome but timid young men—can also be traced to people Wharton knew in New York.

The Age of Innocence is the story of a love affair between a married man, Newland Archer, and the former Ellen Mingott, now estranged from her brutal European husband, Baron Olenski.

Ellen is dark, romantic, cultivated, and bold—the very woman Wharton had longed to be when she was young. Newland's wife, May, personifies the manners and style of "old" New York; she is intelligent, civilized, committed to family traditions, uninterested in taking risks.

Newland loves his wife, but he is frustrated by his safe, predictable life. He longs for something fresh and exciting, and he finds it in Ellen. Restrained by the pressures of custom and family obligation—and by his own timidity—Newland eventually rejects rebellion. He returns to May and to the world of safety and order. Old family values win out against the quest for personal fulfillment.

As Wharton presents it, Newland's decision is understandable, and even praiseworthy. The reader nevertheless gets the sense of missed opportunities, of promising paths forever left unexplored. At the book's end, Ellen has returned to Europe, where at last she establishes herself as an independent person and pursues a life of art and culture. Again, she strongly resembles her creator, Edith Wharton.

When *The Age of Innocence* was published in the fall of 1920, it was an instant success. Reviewers praised the book's story line, its flawless organization, its accurate details, its masterful use of language. It sold more than 100,000 copies.

In 1921 *The Age of Innocence* received the Pulitzer Prize for fiction, the highly prestigious award annually bestowed by Columbia University for the year's best American novel. Wharton was the first woman to receive the prize. (Women writers receiving it in subsequent years have included Pearl Buck [*The Good Earth*], Harper Lee [*To Kill a Mockingbird*], Eudora Welty [*The Optimist's Daughter*], and Alice Walker [*The Color Purple*].)

Wharton was naturally pleased to learn she had won the Pulitzer Prize. She was also amused. The award, according to its citation, was given to the

(text continues on page 98)

Alice Walker, who won the 1983 Pulitzer Prize for her novel, The Color Purple, *was the first black woman to receive the fiction award. Its first female recipient was Edith Wharton.*

Seated at her writing desk at Pavillon Colombe, Wharton works on the manuscript of A
Backward Glance, *the autobiography she published in 1934.*

THE AGE OF INNOCENCE

In this scene from Edith Wharton's Pulitzer Prize-winning novel, Newland Archer, a wealthy young New Yorker, is seated in a brougham (horse-drawn carriage) with Ellen Olenska, the woman he loves. The two are entering Manhattan on a ferryboat. Olenska, whose cousin May is Archer's wife, is separated from her brutal husband. In her conversation with Archer, Olenska mentions "the Gorgon," a mythological monster whose eyes were said to turn anyone looking into them to stone.

I think you're the most honest woman I ever met!" he exclaimed.

"Oh, no—but probably one of the least fussy," she answered, a smile in her voice.

"Call it what you like: you look at things as they are."

"Ah—I've had to. I've had to look at the Gorgon."

"Well—it hasn't blinded you! You've seen that she's just an old bogey like all the others."

"She doesn't blind one; but she dries up one's tears."

The answer checked the pleading on Archer's lips: it seemed to come from depths of experience beyond his reach. The slow advance of the ferryboat had ceased, and her bows bumped against the piles of the slip with a violence that made the brougham stagger, and flung Archer and Madame Olenska against each other. The young man, trembling, felt the pressure of her shoulder and passed his arm around her.

"If you're not blind, then, you must see that this can't last."

"What can't?"

"Our being together—and not together."

"No. You ought not to have come today," she said in an altered voice; and suddenly she turned, flung her arms about him, and pressed her lips to his. At the same moment the carriage began to move, and a gaslight at the head of the slip flashed its light into the window. She drew away, and they sat silent and motionless while the brougham struggled through the congestion of carriages about the ferry landing. As they gained the street Archer began to speak hurriedly.

"Don't be afraid of me: you needn't squeeze yourself back into your corner like that. A stolen kiss isn't what I want. Look, I'm not even trying to touch the sleeve of your jacket. Don't suppose that I don't understand your reasons for not wanting to let this feeling between us dwindle into an ordinary hole-and-corner love affair. I couldn't have spoken like this yesterday, because when we've been apart, and I'm looking forward to seeing you, every thought is burnt up in a great flame. But then you come; and you're so much more than I remembered, and what I want of you is so much more than an hour or two every now and then, with wastes of thirsty waiting between, that I can sit perfectly still beside you like this, with that other vision in my mind, just quietly trusting to it to come true."

For a moment she made no reply; then she asked, hardly above a whisper: "What do you mean by trusting to it to come true?"

"Why—you know it will, don't you?"

"Your vision of you and me together?" She burst into a sudden, hard laugh. "You choose your place well to put it to me!"

"Do you mean because we're in my wife's brougham? Shall we get out and walk, then? I don't suppose you mind a little snow?"

She laughed again, more gently. "No; I shan't get out and walk, because my business is to get to Granny's as quickly as I can. And you'll sit beside me, and we'll look, not at visions, but at realities."

"I don't know what you mean by realities. The only reality to me is this."

She met the words with a long silence, during which the carriage rolled down an obscure side street and then turned into the searching illumination of Fifth Avenue.

" Is it your idea, then, that I should live with you as your mistress—since I can't be your wife?" she asked.

The crudeness of the question startled him: the word was one that women of his class fought shy of, even when their talk flitted closest about the topic. He noticed that Madame Olenska pronounced it as if it had a recognized place in her vocabulary, and he wondered if it had been used familiarly in her presence in the horrible life she had fled from. Her question pulled him up with a jerk, and he floundered.

"I want—I want somehow to get away with you into a world where words like that—categories like that—won't exist. Where we shall be simply two human beings who love each other, who are the whole of life to each other, and nothing else on earth will matter."

She drew a deep sigh that ended in another laugh. "Oh, my dear—where is that country? Have you ever been there?" she asked; and as he remained sullenly dumb she went on, "I know so many who've tried to find it; and believe me, they all got out by mistake at wayside stations: at places like Boulogne, or Pisa, or Monte Carlo—and it wasn't at all different from the old world they'd left, but only rather smaller and dingier and more promiscuous."

He had never heard her speak in such a tone, and he remembered the phrase she had used a little while before.

"Yes, the Gorgon *has* dried your tears," he said.

"Well, she opened my eyes, too; it's a delusion to say that she blinds people. What she does is just the contrary—she fastens their eyelids open, so that they're never again in the blessed darkness. Isn't there a Chinese torture like that? There ought to be. Ah, believe me, it's a miserable little country!"

The carriage had crossed Forty-second Street: May's sturdy brougham horse was carrying them northward as if he had been a Kentucky trotter. Archer choked with the sense of wasted minutes and vain words.

"Then what, exactly, is your plan for us?" he asked.

"For *us*? But there's no *us* in that sense! We're near each other only if we stay far from each other. Then we can be ourselves. Otherwise we're only Newland Archer, the husband of Ellen Olenska's cousin, and Ellen Olenska, the cousin of Newland Archer's wife, trying to be happy behind the backs of the people who trust them."

"Ah, I'm beyond that," he groaned.

"No, you're not! You've never been beyond. And *I* have," she said in a strange voice, "and I know what it looks like there."

He sat silent, dazed with inarticulate pain. Then he groped in the darkness of the carriage for the little bell that signaled orders to the coachman. He remembered that May rang twice when she wished to stop. He pressed the bell, and the carriage drew up beside the curbstone.

"Why are you stopping? This is not Granny's," Madame Olenska exclaimed.

"No: I shall get out here," he stammered, opening the door and jumping to the pavement. By the light of a streetlamp he saw her startled face and the instinctive motion she made to detain him. He closed the door and leaned for a moment in the window.

"You're right: I ought not to have come today," he said, lowering his voice so that the coachman should not hear. She bent forward and seemed about to speak, but he had already called out the order to drive on, and the carriage rolled away while he stood on the corner. The snow was over, and a tingling wind had sprung up, that lashed his face as he stood gazing. Suddenly he felt something stiff and cold on his lashes, and perceived that he had been crying, and that the wind had frozen his tears.

He thrust his hands in his pockets and walked at a sharp pace down Fifth Avenue to his own house.

At the age of 63 Wharton was not only America's most widely acclaimed novelist, she was one of its best paid. Between 1920 and 1924, she earned more than $250,000

(text continued from page 92)

novel that best presented "the wholesome atmosphere of American life and the highest standards of American manners and manhood." For years Wharton had been criticized for creating "sordid" plots and "disagreeable" characters; being rewarded for "wholesomeness" struck her as a choice bit of irony.

Wharton's next novel, *The Glimpses of the Moon*, was published in 1922. It tells the story of an impoverished young couple, Nick and Susy Lansing, who agree to divorce as soon as either gets the chance to marry a wealthy spouse. The two think of themselves as sophisticated and cynical, but in the end they realize they love each other too much to carry out their plan.

Few modern critics consider *The Glimpses of the Moon* one of Wharton's better works. Nor was it admired by its first reviewers, who called the novel "sentimental," "unpersuasive," and "dowdy." It was, however, a runaway best-seller, earning its author $60,000 within a year.

In 1923 *Glimpses* was made into a Hollywood movie. "Talkies" had not yet been invented; the film's dialogue was seen in subtitles. They were written by novelist F. Scott Fitzgerald, who would, three years later, write *The Great Gatsby*. Like the book, the film version of *The Glimpses of the Moon* was hugely successful with the public.

In 1923 Yale University asked Wharton to come to the United States to receive the honorary degree of Doctor of Letters. After living in Europe for the past 10 years, she was reluctant to consider a visit. On the other hand, her books were about Americans and largely read by Americans; she knew it was time she refreshed her knowledge of her native land.

Yale was politely insistent; she was, officials pointed out, the first woman ever so honored by the university. Wharton finally relented, and in late June she received her doctorate in New Haven, Connecticut. Its citation read: "She holds a universally recognized place in the front ranks of the world's living novelists. She has elevated the level of American literature. We are proud that she is an American."

After 11 days in the United States, Wharton recrossed the Atlantic. She had loved—and consumed huge quantities of—vanilla ice cream, a treat unavailable in Europe, but she had come to regard France as her home, and she was glad to be back. She would never again see America.

During the next few years, Wharton continued to entertain friends, to work in her garden, to travel, and to write. *A Son at the Front*, a novel about the war, was published in 1923; *Old New York*, a collection of stories, in 1924; *The Mother's Recompense*, a novel about parents and children, in 1925.

As always, Wharton spent much time with her old friend, Walter Berry. In 1926 the pair took a leisurely trip through Italy. It was to be their final journey together. The following year Berry suffered a severe stroke. Wharton watched over her beloved companion of so many years during the last days of his life. The day before he died, she held him in her arms and talked of their many happy times together.

"No words can tell of my desolation,"

Famed as the chronicler of the "Jazz Age," novelist F. Scott Fitzgerald wrote the screenplay for The Glimpses of the Moon, *the popular film based on Wharton's 1922 novel.*

In a scene from the hugely successful 1929 stage presentation of Wharton's The Age of Innocence, *Katherine Cornell (right) plays Ellen Olenska opposite Edna Gray's May Archer.*

she wrote to a friend after Berry's death. "He had been to me in turn all that one being can be to another in love, in friendship, in understanding." Walter Berry was interred in Versailles; the next day, Wharton wrote in her diary, "The stone closed over all my life."

A few months later, Wharton received more sad news, but this time her grief was bittersweet rather than devastating. Teddy Wharton had died at the age of 79. Edith Wharton had not heard from her former husband for more than 10 years, although from time to time friends would report that he still seemed unable to understand what had happened to his marriage. "Puss shouldn't have done that to me," he would say vaguely. "I am thankful," she said when she heard of his death, "to think of him at peace after all these weary, agitated years."

In September 1928 Wharton published *The Children*, a rather sentimental tale about a middle-aged bachelor and a brood of rich but neglected half brothers and sisters. In a situation reminiscent of the appearance of *The Glimpses of the Moon*, the critics strongly disapproved of the book, and the public loved it. It was, in fact, the most financially successful work ever produced by Wharton, earning her almost $100,000.

Edith Wharton's final novels were *Hudson River Bracketed* (1929) and *The Gods Arrive* (1932). Although they were among her five favorites (the others were *The Custom of the Country*, *Summer*, and *The Children*), they were only modestly successful with critics and readers. After their publication, Wharton began to work on her autobiography, which she had been considering for a number of years.

A Backward Glance was published in 1934. It is an account of Wharton's ancestors, her parents and their courtship, the places—New York, Newport, Paris—where she lived. It contains sharply etched portraits of Henry James and several other notable Wharton friends.

Wharton, who was 70 when she began her autobiography, was distrustful of her memory. She would hate to repeat, she jokingly told a friend, "the

pathetic case of the little old lady confessing over and over again her one adultery." Her fears turned out to be groundless: the book is as insightful and crisp as anything she ever wrote.

The first words of *A Backward Glance* are, "There is no such thing as growing old." The passing years touched Edith Wharton, of course, as they did everyone else. But in one sense she never aged, perhaps because she hated ruts, despised what she called "the deathly process of doing the same thing in the same way at the same hour day after day."

At the age of 72 Wharton was off on a trip to Wales, then to a music festival in Salzburg, Austria. She had, she told a friend, a "restless desire to tick off as many places as possible before the crash."

In a letter to a friend in 1936, when she was 74 years old, Wharton wrote, "I wish I knew what people meant when they say they find 'emptiness' in this wonderful adventure of living, which seems to me to pile up its glories like a horizon-wide sunset as the light declines. I'm afraid I'm an incorrigible life-lover, life-wonderer, and adventurer."

In the summer of 1936 Wharton treated herself to another trip abroad, this time to England, where she saw a performance of Mozart's opera *Don Giovanni* at a music festival. She was in fine health and as full of enthusiasm

Toote   Choumai

Wharton plays with two of her beloved pets outside her home near Paris. "I am secretly afraid of all animals," she wrote in a 1924 diary entry, "except dogs."

for company and conversation as ever.

Soon after her return from England, she was entertaining friends at Pavillon Colombe, her home outside Paris. One of the younger guests noted that Wharton's prized goldfish had been at the estate when she bought it and asked how old they were. Told they were at least 75, he was amazed. How would it feel, he wondered aloud, to be so ancient? Edith Wharton, who had just celebrated her 75th birthday, smiled. "It feels pretty good," she said, "when you get to it."

A few months later, however, Wharton began to have repeated spells of dizziness, and in June 1937 she suffered a major stroke. The next two months were peaceful; she spent her days at her handsome house near Paris, talking gently with old friends about past adventures.

Aware that she had little time left, Wharton was serene. She gave careful directions for the disposition of articles not mentioned in her will, specifically requesting that all her clothing go to a friend "who hasn't much money to buy dresses."

Edith Wharton died on August 11, 1937. A contingent of devoted friends, accompanied by an honor guard of war veterans, transported her casket to the Versailles cemetery where she had interred Walter Berry. It was lowered into the ground next to his.

Edith Wharton wrote 17 novels, dozens of short stories, a large number of magazine articles and travel pieces, many poems, several works on architecture and gardens, and an autobiography. Not everything she produced is considered first-rate today, but some of her short stories and novels—notably *The House of Mirth*, *The Age of Innocence*, *Ethan Frome*, *Summer*, and *The Custom of the Country*—are undisputed masterpieces.

More incisively than any writer of her era, Wharton presented the conflict between personal independence and social convention. With clarity, irony, and wit, she portrayed the world into which she was born, a world in which a new, brash class of affluent Americans competed for dominance with the established families of the "old" society.

A meticulous writer who reworked and revised every manuscript until it said exactly what she meant, Wharton was a master at describing the situation of women at the end of the 19th century and the early part of the 20th century. She was not part of the feminist movement of her time but, as novelist and critic Marilyn French has pointed out, "feminist concerns do appear in her work."

Wharton's "strongest and most sympathetically considered characters are women who risk," says French. "These women have moral courage, something even Wharton's most sympathetic men lack. They are not passive victims of their lives, although there is no question of their triumphing over circumstances; what they do is live their lives out fully, by feeling and thinking through whatever occurs, by refusing to blind themselves. They risk discovering their own dark sides, their sexuality, their guilt, their jealousy."

Edith Wharton's "richest gifts," writes biographer and literary critic Cynthia Griffin Wolff, "devolve from her uncompromising search for truth and from the honesty with which she confronted the complex emotional and passional life which we all experience. Her novels record timeless truths, and it is this fact above all that continues to make them meaningful and important." R. W. B. Lewis, Wharton's most important biographer, perhaps best sums up the impact of her books. "With their muted subtleties, their preciseness of allusion, and above all the compassion for the wounded or thwarted life that flows through them," he writes, they "are among the handsomest achievements in our literature."

Always a passionate gardener, Wharton enjoys Ste. Claire's flowery terrace in 1933. "My old fibres," she once said, "have been so closely interwoven with all these roots and tendrils."

THE WRITINGS OF EDITH WHARTON

NOVELS AND NOVELLAS

THE TOUCHSTONE, 1900.

THE VALLEY OF DECISION, 1902.

SANCTUARY, 1903.

THE HOUSE OF MIRTH, 1905.

MADAME DE TREYMES, 1907.

THE FRUIT OF THE TREE, 1907.

ETHAN FROME, 1911.

THE REEF, 1912.

THE CUSTOM OF THE COUNTRY, 1913.

THE SUMMER, 1917.

THE MARNE, 1918.

THE AGE OF INNOCENCE, 1920.

THE GLIMPSES OF THE MOON, 1922.

A SON AT THE FRONT, 1923.

OLD NEW YORK, 1924.

THE MOTHER'S RECOMPENSE, 1925.

TWILIGHT SLEEP, 1927.

THE CHILDREN, 1928.

HUDSON RIVER BRACKETED, 1929.

THE GODS ARRIVE, 1932.

THE BUCCANEERS, 1938 (unfinished).

SHORT STORIES AND POETRY

THE GREATER INCLINATION, 1899.

CRUCIAL INSTANCES, 1901.

THE DESCENT OF MAN, AND OTHER STORIES, 1904.

THE HERMIT AND THE WILD WOMAN AND OTHER STORIES, 1908.

ARTEMIS TO ACTAEON AND OTHER VERSE, 1909.

TALES OF MEN AND GHOSTS, 1910.

XINGU AND OTHER STORIES, 1916.

HERE AND BEYOND, 1926.

TWELVE POEMS, 1926.

CERTAIN PEOPLE, 1930.

HUMAN NATURE, 1933.

THE WORLD OVER, 1936.

GHOSTS, 1937.

NONFICTION

THE DECORATION OF HOUSES (with Ogden Codman, Jr.), 1897.

ITALIAN VILLAS AND THEIR GARDENS, 1904.

ITALIAN BACKGROUNDS, 1905.

A MOTOR-FLIGHT THROUGH FRANCE, 1908.

FIGHTING FRANCE, FROM DUNKERQUE TO BELFORT, 1915.

FRENCH WAYS AND THEIR MEANING, 1919.

IN MOROCCO, 1920.

THE WRITING OF FICTION, 1925.

A BACKWARD GLANCE, 1934.

FURTHER READING

Auchincloss, Louis. *Edith Wharton: A Woman in Her Time.* New York: Viking, 1971.

Bell, Millicent. *Edith Wharton and Henry James.* New York: Brazillier, 1965.

Howe, Irving, ed. *Edith Wharton: A Collection of Critical Essays.* Englewood Cliffs, NJ: Prentice Hall, 1962.

Lewis, R. W. B. *Edith Wharton: A Biography.* New York: Fromm International, 1985.

Nevius, Blake. *Edith Wharton: A Study of Her Fiction.* Berkeley: University of California Press, 1953.

Woolf, Cynthia Griffin. *A Feast of Words: The Triumph of Edith Wharton.* New York: Oxford University Press, 1977.

CHRONOLOGY

Jan. 24, 1862	Born Edith Newbold Jones in New York City
1866–72	Tours Europe with family
1879	Makes debut into New York society
1885	Marries Edward R. Wharton
1890	Publishes first fiction, "Mrs. Manstey's View," a short story
1897	Publishes *The Decoration of Houses*
1899	Publishes first story collection, *The Greater Inclination*
1902	Publishes first novel, *The Valley of Decision*
1903	Begins lifelong friendship with novelist Henry James
1905	Publishes *The House of Mirth*
1907	Meets Morton Fullerton in Paris
1911	Publishes *Ethan Frome*
1912	Moves to France
1913	Divorces Edward Wharton
	Publishes *The Custom of the Country*
1914	Organizes refugee aid after outbreak of World War I
1916	Awarded France's Cross of the Legion of Honor
1917	Publishes *Summer*
1920	Publishes *The Age of Innocence*
1921	Receives Pulitzer Prize
1923	Receives honorary doctorate from Yale University
1934	Publishes autobiography, *A Backward Glance*
Aug. 11, 1937	Dies in Paris

INDEX

PICTURE CREDITS

AP/Wide World: pp. 44, 86;   The Bettmann Archive: pp. 17, 22, 23,
24, 30, 37, 50, 52, 59, 60, 67, 70, 71, 74, 75, 77, 78, 79, 80, 83, 85, 88,
89, 99;   Culver Pictures: pp. 35, 36, 51, 57, 98;   New York Public
Library, Billy Rose Theatre Collection, Astor, Lennox and Tilden
Foundation: pp. 66, 100;   UPI/Bettmann Newsphotos: pp. 76,
92;   Yale Collection of American Literature, Beinecke Library: pp.
2, 12, 14, 15, 16, 18, 20, 25, 26, 27, 29, 33, 35, 38, 39, 40, 41, 42, 43, 46,
48, 49, 53, 54, 62, 64, 68, 69, 73, 81, 82, 90, 91, 93, 102, 104

William Leach is a fellow at The New York Institute for the Humanities at New York University, and author of *True Love and Perfect Union, The Feminist Reform of Sex and Society*. He has been awarded fellowships from several institutions, including the National Endowment for the Humanities, the Guggenheim Foundation, and the Woodrow Wilson International Center for Scholars.

❖   ❖   ❖

Matina S. Horner is president of Radcliffe College and associate professor of psychology and social relations at Harvard University. She is best known for her studies of women's motivation, achievement, and personality development. Dr. Horner serves on several national boards and advisory councils, including those of the National Science Foundation, Time Inc., and the Women's Research and Education Institute. She earned her B. A. from Bryn Mawr College and Ph.D. from the University of Michigan, and holds honorary degrees from many colleges and universities, including Mount Holyoke, Smith, Tufts, and the University of Pennsylvania.